Wine, Food & Friends

Karen MacNeil

Oxmoor House®

Library of Congress Control Number: 2006929980

ISBN-13: 978-0-8487-3122-9
ISBN-10: 0-8487-3122-0
Printed in the United States of America
First printing 2006

Oxmoor House, Inc.
Editor in Chief: Nancy Fitzpatrick Wyatt
Executive Editor: Katherine M. Eakin
Copy Chief: Allison Long Lowery

Wine, Food & Friends

Author: Karen MacNeil with
   the editors of *Cooking Light*
Editor: Anne C. Cain, M.P.H., M.S., R.D.
Senior Copy Editor: L. Amanda Owens
Contributing Copy Editor: Jacqueline Giovanelli
Editorial Assistants: Julie Boston,
   Brigette Gaucher
Senior Designer: Melissa Jones Clark
Director of Production: Laura Lockhart
Senior Production Manager: Greg A. Amason
Production Assistant: Faye Porter Bonner
Test Kitchens Director: Elizabeth Tyler Austin
Assistant Director, Test Kitchens: Julie Christopher
Food Stylist: Kelley Self Wilton
Test Kitchens Professionals: Nicole Lee Faber,
   Kathleen Royal Phillips
Photography Director: Jim Bathie
Senior Photo Stylist: Kay E. Clarke
Photo Stylist: Katherine Eckert

Contributors
Designer: Rita Yerby
Interns: Ashley Leath, Caroline Markunas,
   Mary Katherine Pappas, Vanessa Rusch Thomas
Indexer: Mary Ann Laurens
Photographers: Lee Harrelson, Michael Weschler
   (cover photo and pages 19, 22, 58, and 144)
Photo Stylist: Katie Stoddard
Proofreaders: Dolores Hydock, Barzella Papa

Cooking Light®
Editor in Chief: Mary Kay Culpepper
Executive Editor: Billy R. Sims
Art Director: Susan Waldrip Dendy
Managing Editor: Maelynn Cheung
Senior Food Editor: Alison Mann Ashton
Senior Editor: Anamary Pelayo
Features Editor: Phillip Rhodes
Projects Editor: Mary Simpson Creel, M.S., R.D.
Food Editor: Ann Taylor Pittman
Associate Food Editors: Julianna Grimes Bottcher,
   Timothy Q. Cebula
Assistant Food Editor: Kathy C. Kitchens, R.D.
Assistant Editor: Cindy Hatcher
Test Kitchens Director: Vanessa Taylor Johnson
Senior Food Stylist: Kellie Gerber Kelley
Food Stylist: M. Kathleen Kanen
Test Kitchens Professionals: Sam Brannock,
   Kathryn Conrad, Mary H. Drennen,
   Jan Jacks Moon, Tiffany Vickers, Mike Wilson
Assistant Art Director: Maya Metz Logue
Senior Designers: Fernande Bondarenko,
   J. Shay McNamee
Designer: Brigette Mayer
Senior Photographer: Randy Mayor
Senior Photo Stylist: Cindy Barr
Photo Stylists: Melanie J. Clarke, Jan Gautro
Studio Assistant: Celine Chenoweth

Contributors
Photographer: Becky Luigart-Stayner
Photo Stylists: Lydia DeGaris-Pursell,
   Fonda Shaia
Recipe Developers: Maureen Callahan,
   Martha Condra, Lorrie Hulston Corvin,
   Sandra Granseth, Lia Huber,
   Jean Kressy, Donata Maggipinto,
   Krista Ackerbloom Montgomery,
   Diane Morgan, Kitty Morse, Cynthia Nicholson,
   Mark Scarbrough, Elizabeth Taliaferro,
   Robin Vitetta-Miller, Bruce Weinstein,
   Joanne Weir

acknowledgments

There are many people who helped make *Wine, Food & Friends* a reality and success. Above all, to editors Anne Cain and Nancy Wyatt, designer Rita Yerby, and publisher Brian Carnahan at Oxmoor House—thank you for being a joy to work with. To the editors at *Cooking Light* and publisher Chris Allen—a toast to many more years of working together. I owe my assistant Catherine Seda an enormous amount of gratitude for her hard work on this book; also Robbin Rutherford, who helped the project take shape. I want to thank my colleagues at the Culinary Institute of America and especially chef David Katz, who helped me test recipes and stuck around to taste them with all sorts of wines. To my outrageously funny, serious, and sensational producers at New River Media/Team, I adore you all—especially Andrew Walworth, Ernie Crow, Christina Mazzanti, Brittany Huckabee, John Sorensen, Sydnye White, Matthew Faraci, Brian Buckley, and Dave Goulding (the camera wasn't rolling; I was just talking to Dave, wasn't I?). And to the inimitable Scott Puritz, who mastered wine in a lightening flash, thank you forever for being the visionary.

—KM

To my daughter, Emma, who swirled

her milk and began taking notes on its flavor

when she was three years old.

And to Debbie, my "sister," who's always

loved everything I've cooked and

every wine I've opened.

contents

I've come to realize a central truth about wine—namely, that it is, at its most elemental core, simply liquid flavor.

welcome!

While interviewing a famous chef several years ago, I happened to ask if he thought he knew more about wine than most winemakers know about food. He paused for a second and then chided, "Karen, what a ridiculous question!"

"Why so?" I asked.

"Because if you care about flavor," he replied gently, "what difference does it make if it's solid or liquid in your mouth?"

That response was an epiphany for me, for it captured what I've come to realize is the central truth about wine—namely, that it is, at its most elemental core, simply liquid flavor. The idea is comforting, isn't it? It means that just as one doesn't need to be a food scientist to be passionate and knowledgeable about good food, one also doesn't need to understand enology or viticulture to be passionate and knowledgeable about good wine. In fact, food and wine are not only inseparable, but also basically the same: They are flavor. Which is why, if you develop a passion for one of them, it's so easy to fall for the other, too. I fell in love with both about thirty years ago, and in the process forged a career. It was this passion for wine and food that ultimately led in 2004 to the launch of my first television series on public television, *Wine, Food & Friends with Karen MacNeil.* And that, in turn, sparked the creation of this book—a book that I hope you'll find effortless to use and full of good ideas, a book that will inspire you to be swept away into the endless pleasures of wine and food.

The featured menus are organized by season because seasonal foods are inherently compelling for any cook. The wines that I suggest as fabulous partners for the recipes are personal favorites, and I think you'll enjoy knowing about them. However, if your wine shop doesn't carry the wine listed, don't worry. Simply buy another wine of the same type. So, for example, if you can't find Chappellet Merlot, another merlot of about the same price will work fine. I explain the thinking behind the pairings so that you'll find it easy to "marry well." At the top of each recipe, I've again listed the wine intended to pair with it so if you take the recipe with you when you shop, you'll know which wine to buy.

People who love wine and food inevitably become friends. So visit **winefoodandfriends.com,** see what we're up to next, and let us hear from you.

Gratefully,

Karen MacNeil

wine price key

It's always helpful to have an idea of prices when you're deciding on the wines to serve. Certainly, there are many affordable high-quality wines; there are also some that are worth splurging on. As you read the wine notes with each menu, reference the following symbols:

$ **$7 to $15**
a great deal

$$ **$15 to $25**
moderately priced

$$$ **$25 to $35**
moderately expensive

$$$$ **over $35**
expensive

$$$$$ **over $75**
very expensive, but may be rare, extraordinary, and a once-in-a-lifetime experience

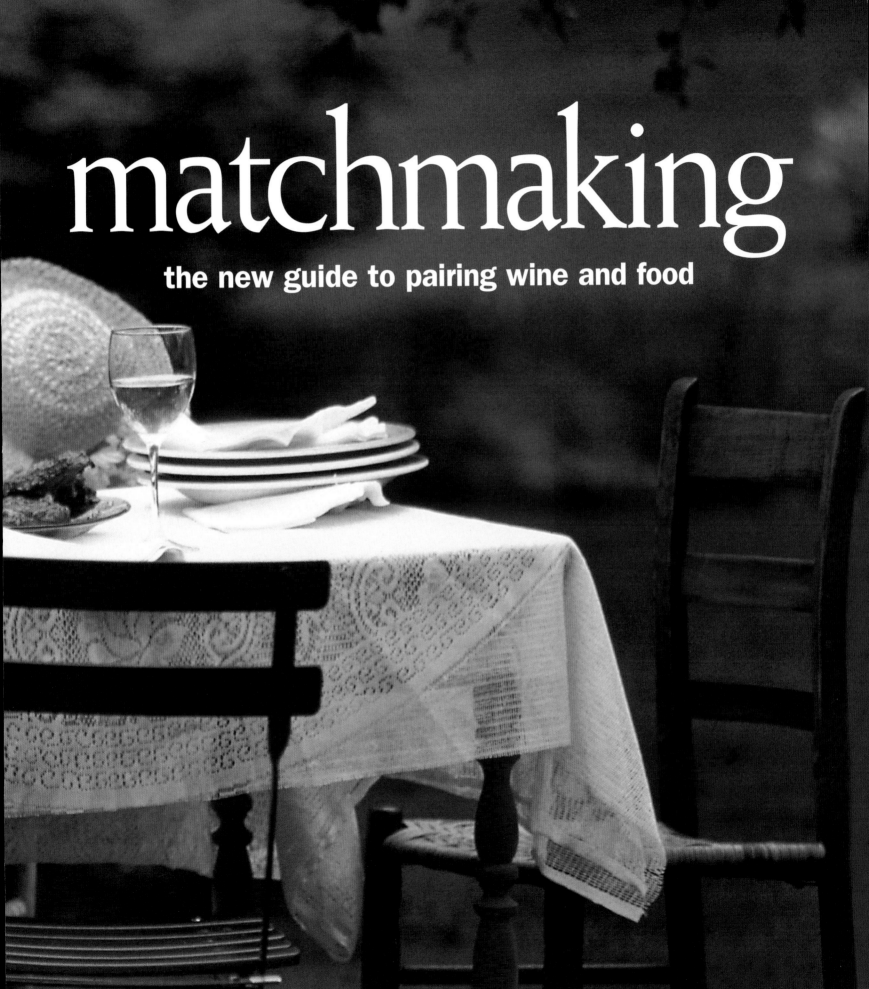

matchmaking

the new guide to pairing wine and food

miraculous matches

from its inception some nine thousand years ago, wine has had a constant, delicious companion: food. In fact, in Europe, where wine was born, the connection between the two is so intimate that it doesn't even draw a distinction. There, wine *is* food. With the exception of breakfast, wine is on the table with every meal.

Given such familiarity, you'd think Europeans would be masters at matching food and wine—being the first and most experienced at it. Interestingly, just the opposite is true. Historically, Europeans drank locally made wine and ate a limited repertoire of local dishes. There was no choice and, therefore, nothing to think about.

A brave new world

Dinners made in modern kitchens reveal that the situation is now very different. Penne with tomatoes and basil served one night might be followed by a ginger-spiked Asian noodle dish the next ... and by meat loaf and mashed potatoes the next. And as for the wines, it's simply astounding how many choices are available. A typical wine shop in the United States may have from 500 to 5,000 different wines from all over the world. This remarkable and far-reaching diversity of food and wines has ushered in a brave new world of pairing them. At no other time in history have the possibilities been so thrilling, so delicious, so limitless. The question, of course, is how exactly does one go about pairing them?

For me, the answer is to rely on instinct and a few guidelines—but no rigid rules. That approach may seem odd for a book

The remarkable and far-reaching diversity of food and wines has ushered in a brave new world of pairing them.

Lemon-Shallot Scallops, page 95

Pork Cassoulet, page 180

whose subject, after all, is pairing wine and food. But as every wine and food lover has witnessed, rules (if they even exist) simply aren't necessary. There have always been great dinners during which no one consciously paired the wine and food, and yet the evening turned out to be a huge success. If experience teaches us anything, it's that the right mood is probably at least as important as the "right" wine and food.

The "wow!" moments

On the other hand, it's most certainly true that extraordinary flavor affinities *do* exist. And when they happen, it's like throwing a switch in the brain—we just know it. At that moment, the harmonic convergence of wine and food is so exceptional that one is transported into some other world of almost unreal flavor sensations. Wow moments such as these are extremely addictive. Any wine and food lover is powerless to resist them and intrigued to pursue them—or at least have fun trying.

The world of flavor is anything but finite; combinations, therefore, are theoretically incalculable. When all the molecular flavors in a dish are swirled together with all the molecular flavors in a wine, almost anything can happen.

Complex considerations

Imbedded here, of course, is the realization that flavor is almost never a singular idea. Which is why, I guess, I'm always a little amused to be asked something along the lines of which wine goes with chicken. Chicken in curried coconut milk sauce? Chicken mopped with a sweet barbecue glaze? Roasted chicken with garlic slipped under the skin? Chicken salad? In each of these cases, the chicken might well be the least significant factor in determining the perfect wine. It may be surpassed by flavors of other ingredients, seasonings, and spices, plus the myriad flavors and textures created by the cooking technique (the char of a grill, the sweetness of roasting) as well as by the simplest variable of all: temperature. Cold chicken, alas, tastes different than hot. And the final straw of all is subjectivity. Taste is intimate and ultimately personal.

For many years what I came to think of as the "intellectual messiness" of wine-and-food pairing made me want to avoid the concept altogether. Wine and food were my constant inspiration and pleasure. I made my living writing about them. The notion that there were rules for putting them together seemed to be, at the very least, joyless.

1+1=3

So I stood in the kitchen, night after night, and cooked and tasted wine. (In order to teach and write about wine, I sample about 12 wines a night—spitting out, of course.) Several years ago, I noticed that I'd begun to take notes on not just the dishes and wines, but also on the effect they had on each other. Sometimes, a wine would actually make a dish taste better, though the wine's flavor remained the same. At other times, the opposite was true: The dish would make the wine taste better, and the flavor of the dish remained the same. Occasionally, almost miraculously, the wine *and* food would improve because of each other. And when this kind of partnership happens, it isn't subtle. A great match works both ways. It's 1 plus 1 equals 3. It is fireworks.

Ultimately, I came to see the intentional pairing of wine and food in a new light. I realized that it never could—and perhaps never should—be a science. It belongs instead to the realm of the senses. Great matches are born from instinct and imagination. They are the captivating result of drinking different kinds of wines with different kinds of dishes and then paying attention to the principles that emerge. After years of doing just that, I've discovered the following 14 pairing principles. They are fairly simple ideas, meant as a starting point to compel you to take out a corkscrew and to tempt you into the kitchen. For, in the end, wine and food are the most inevitable and accessible of pleasures. They are a necessary component of life. They are our guide, our lure, our oasis.

If experience teaches us anything, it's that the right mood is probably at least as important as the "right" wine and food.

Serve a high-quality but simple dish, such as grilled beef tenderloin, with a complex wine.

A humble dish, such as beef stew, doesn't need an expensive wine to accompany it.

pairing principles

Consider complexity.

Complex wines taste best when paired with foods that are simply prepared. A complex wine is one that draws you into it, compelling you to taste it again and again in order to experience its multitude of flavors and aromas, which reveal themselves sequentially over time. By definition, a complex wine is not knowable in one sip. Complexity is a hallmark of the greatest (and most expensive) wines in the world and is often fairly subtle. To experience it fully, the taster can't have other flavors competing for attention. For this reason, many of the greatest Bordeaux or California cabernet sauvignons are served with a high-quality but simple dish, such as a fine steak.

Consider intensity and weight.

Besides the intensity of flavors, the heaviness of the dish and the weight of the wine should be in harmony. The weight of a wine is known as the wine's body. A light-bodied wine feels about as weighty as skim milk in your mouth, a medium-bodied wine feels like whole milk, and a full-bodied wine feels like half-and-half. Some full-bodied wines, such as Australian shirazes, can be as weighty and dense as pancake syrup. Such wines are totally out of sync with a light dish, such as a fillet of sole.

Pair humble with humble and great with great.

Wines and foods of the same "status" have a natural bond. A humble dish, such as a pot roast, doesn't need— indeed, doesn't even feel right with—a $100 pinot noir accompanying it. On the other hand, an expensive standing prime rib roast is far more satisfying when it's served with a wine of commensurate greatness.

Spicy dishes with lots of texture pair extremely well with bold wines, such as a gewürztraminer.

Pairing roasted pork and a crisp riesling creates a delicious food-and-wine contrast.

Match delicate to delicate and robust to robust.

Delicate wine flavors deserve delicate food flavors, and by the same token robust wines are enhanced by robust foods. Generally speaking, a delicately flavored wine ends up tasting like water if you serve it with a dramatically spiced or piquant dish. On the other hand, dishes with bold, spicy, hot flavors are perfectly cut out for bold, spicy wines. This is one reason many Tex-Mex dishes work so well with zinfandel, as well as why certain "high-tactile" Thai dishes, with lots of heat from chiles and piquancy from such ingredients as garlic and ginger, are so good with outrageously fruity gewürztraminers.

Decide if you want to mirror flavors or to create contrasts.

All pairings are ultimately based on complements and/or contrasts. Complementary pairings are based on foods and wines that mirror one another in flavor, such as a chowder and a chardonnay. Both the chowder and chardonnay are thick, rich, buttery, soft, and creamy. But some of the most delicious and intriguing matches are based on the opposite strategy of contrast. With roasted pork and riesling, for example, the pork is meaty, dense, and rich, while the riesling is fruity, crisp, and lean. As counterpoints, they create a delicious seesaw: A bite of the rich pork makes you want a sip of the refreshing wine, and a sip of the wine makes you want a bite of the pork.

Work with flavor affinities.

Despite the individuality of taste, certain natural flavor affinities exist—work with them. For example, most people agree that coffee and cream have an affinity for each other and that chocolate and basil do not. In many cases, we don't need actual experience to suspect an affinity (or the lack thereof); we have instincts, and instincts are usually reliable. Most people have probably never tried the aforementioned chocolate with basil, and yet the very idea probably produces shudders. Similarly, given an oily food, such as smoked salmon, a tannic red wine strikes many of us as a poor partner. On the other hand, the clean, crisp, bracing freshness of sparkling wine seems just right. Instinct for flavor affinity is hard to explain, but every good cook knows it exists.

All pairings are ultimately based on complements and/or contrasts.

Tangy goat cheese in a salad is a good match for equally tangy sauvignon blanc.

Chianti tastes good with tomato-based sauces because the acid in the wine mirrors the acid in the tomatoes.

Incorporate bridge ingredients.

Certain ingredients—known as bridges—can make the tie between a wine and food more seamless. For example, adding crumbled goat cheese to a salad makes that salad a better match for sauvignon blanc because the cheese and wine share similar tangy flavors. Goat cheese becomes a bridge for connecting the flavors of the salad with the flavors of the wine. Adding black peppercorns to a sauce helps bridge that sauce to a peppery wine, such as a syrah.

Seek out acidity.

High-acid wines are generally easier to pair with a wide variety of foods than low-acid wines. Acidity gives wine liveliness and vivacity. High-acid wines act like a knife, cutting through the flavors of other foods and leaving the palate refreshed and ready for the next bite. Some familiar examples of high-acid whites are riesling, sauvignon blanc, Chablis, Champagne, and sparkling wines. Pinot noir and sangiovese (the main grape in Chianti) are good examples of red wines with relatively high acidity.

High-acid wines are generally easier to pair with a wide variety of foods than low-acid wines.

assets of wines with good acidity

• High acidity in a wine often balances a food's saltiness (which is why Champagne is so good with caviar).

• High acidity in a wine is a great complement to mineraliness or brininess in a food (which is why Chablis and Muscadet are so good with oysters).

• High acidity in a wine is a terrific counterpoint to smoked foods (which is why riesling is so good with smoked trout).

• High acidity in a wine cuts through the palate-coating effect of olive oil (which is why Chianti tastes good with so many olive oil-laced pasta dishes).

• High acidity in a wine mirrors and complements foods with relatively high acid contents, such as tomatoes, vinegars, and citrus fruits (which is why that same Chianti tastes so good with tomato-based spaghetti sauce).

Fruity wines possess a cornucopia of fruit flavors.

Balance saltiness in such foods as cheese with a touch of sweetness.

Incorporate fruit.

Fruitiness in wine has natural synergy with fruitiness in food. Gewürztraminer, muscat, viognier, and riesling are the most fruity whites. Gamay (the grape that makes Beaujolais) and Australian shiraz are examples of fruity reds. Dishes with a significant fruit component—such as pork with sautéed apples, barbecue chicken with apricot glaze, and beef stew with prunes—often pair beautifully with fruity wines.

Remember rosé.

Often overlooked, rosé wines are wonderful served with a surprising range of dishes. Rosés have the earthy, bold fruit character of red wines and the light, fresh acidity of white wines. This duality is an enormous asset in pairing certain foods—especially highly pungent foods, such as those containing garlic, an ingredient that has a persistence on the palate that can swamp other flavors and virtually obliterate their nuances. As a result, many white and red wines simply taste neutral, hollow, and dull when consumed with garlicky dishes. On the other hand, rosé wines have an affinity with garlic that's truly remarkable. In the Mediterranean, for example, garlicky sauces (such as aïoli) are always served with a chilled dry rosé.

Pair salty and sweet.

Salty foods dull the flavor of many wines, making them taste neutral. For example, most cheeses, which are high in salt, make fine red wines taste hollow. As a broad rule of thumb, cheeses are generally better paired with high-acid white wines. Probably one of the best-kept secrets in the world of pairing wine and food is how majestic triple-cream cheeses taste with sparkling wines and Champagne. Saltiness is also an important consideration for dishes seasoned with significant amounts of soy sauce. As noted, acidity in wine can counterbalance a food's saltiness; another brilliant strategy is to juxtapose that saltiness with a touch of sweetness. Try an Asian stir-fry seasoned with soy sauce with an off-dry American gewürztraminer. This is the principle behind the great traditional pairing of Stilton cheese (something salty) with Port (something sweet).

High-tannin wines taste best with dense foods that are high in both protein and fat, such as red meat.

With dessert—and sweet foods in general—the wine should always be sweeter than the dessert.

Think about tannin.

Wines with a lot of tannin (a compound that comes from grape skins and seeds), such as a top-notch cabernet sauvignon, taste best with dense foods that are high in both protein and fat, such as red meat. Some grape varieties—such as cabernet sauvignon, merlot, petite sirah, and nebbiolo—are naturally high in this compound. Tannin acts as the wine's structure, or skeleton, so wines that are high in tannin are usually described as "big." Tannin also has both a flavor and feel. Tannin tastes bitter (like dark chocolate or espresso) and feels dry (like fine-gauge sandpaper). As a result, tannin is beautifully offset by red meat's protein and fat.

Reconsider oak.

Wines with a lot of oak flavor, such as California chardonnays, are generally the hardest to pair with a wide variety of foods. With many dishes, that oakiness comes across so strongly that the wine tastes hard and flat. Oaky wines—in particular chardonnays—often need a bridge to connect them to food. Toasted nuts, brown butter, caramel, and sesame oil are excellent bridges to an oaky chardonnay.

Don't forget dessert.

With dessert—and sweet foods in general—the accompanying wine should always be sweeter than the dessert. A good example is a fruit tart served with a glass of Sauternes, the honeyed wine of Bordeaux. The marriage works because the dessert wine is sweeter than the dessert itself. If the dessert is sweeter, then the wine tastes dull and blank—which is why wedding cake makes an expensive dry Champagne taste like tap water.

Probably one of the best-kept secrets in the world of pairing wine and food is how majestic triple-cream cheeses taste with sparkling wines and Champagne.

A SHORTCUT GUIDE TO WINE-AND-FOOD PAIRING

Here are six top varietals and some foods that are delicious served with them.

Wine Varietal	Herbs and Spices	Vegetables	Fish and Shellfish	Meats	Cheeses	Good Bridges
SAUVIGNON BLANC	Basil, bay leaf, cilantro, dill, fennel, lemongrass, marjoram, mint, parsley, savory, thyme	Carrots, eggplant, most green vegetables (lettuces, snow peas, zucchini), tomatoes	Sea bass, snapper, sole, swordfish, trout, tuna, clams, mussels, oysters, scallops, shrimp	Chicken, game birds, turkey	Buffalo mozzarella, feta, fontina, goat, Parmigiano-Reggiano, ricotta, Swiss	Bell peppers (fresh, roasted), capers, citrus (lemon, lime, orange), fennel, garlic, green figs, leeks, olives, sour cream, tomatoes (fresh, sun-dried)
CHARDONNAY	Basil, clove, tarragon, thyme	Corn, mushrooms, potatoes, pumpkin, squash	Grouper, halibut, monkfish, salmon, swordfish, tuna, crab, lobster, scallops, shrimp	Chicken, pork, turkey, veal	Brie, camembert, Monterey Jack, Swiss	Apples, avocado, bacon, butter, citrus (lemon juice, lemon zest), coconut milk, cream, Dijon mustard, milk, nuts (almonds, cashews, toasted hazelnuts, pine nuts), pancetta, pears, polenta, tropical fruits (mango, papaya, pineapple), vanilla
RIESLING	Chile pepper, cilantro, dill, five-spice, ginger, lemongrass, nutmeg, parsley	Carrots, corn, onions (roasted, sautéed), parsnips	Smoked fish (salmon, trout), snapper, sole, trout, crab, scallops	Chicken, game birds, pork	Emmenthal, Gouda	Apricots (dried, fresh), citrus (citrus zest, lime, orange), dried fruits (figs, plums, raisins), peaches, tropical fruits (mango, papaya)
PINOT NOIR	Basil, black pepper, cinnamon, clove, fennel, five-spice, oregano, rosemary, star anise, thyme	Beets, eggplant, mushrooms	Salmon (baked, grilled, sautéed), tuna	Beef, chicken, game birds, lamb, liver, rabbit, squab, turkey, veal	Aged Cheddar, Brie	Beets, butter, Dijon mustard, dried fruits (cherries, cranberries, plums, raisins), mushrooms, onions (roasted, sautéed), pomegranates, pomegranate molasses, shallots, tea, cooked tomatoes, truffles
SYRAH | SHIRAZ	Allspice, chile pepper, coriander, cumin, five-spice, pepper, rosemary, sage	Eggplant, onions (roasted, sautéed), root vegetables	Blackened "meaty" fish (salmon, tuna)	Bacon, duck, lamb, pancetta, pheasant, quail, sausage, short ribs, squab, venison	Cheddar, goat, Gouda, Gruyère	Black figs, black licorice, black olives, black pepper, cherries (fresh, dried), chocolate/cocoa
CABERNET SAUVIGNON	Juniper, oregano, rosemary, sage, savory, thyme	Mushrooms, potatoes, root vegetables	None	Beef (roasts, grilled steak), duck, lamb, venison	Camembert, cantal, carmody, aged Gouda, aged Jack	Balsamic vinegar, blackberries, black olives, black pepper, butter, cassis, cherries (fresh, dried), cream, currants, roasted red pepper, toasted nuts (pecans, walnuts)

wine-and-recipe selection guide

Here's a list of some of the types of wine in this book
and the recipes I've paired them with.

WHITES

CHARDONNAY AND WHITE BURGUNDY

White Bean and Bacon Dip with Rosemary Pita Chips	page 62
Succotash Salad	page 65
Lemon-Shallot Scallops	page 95
Pear-Cheese Strata	page 106
Raisin-Rosemary Rye Bread	page 109
Spiced Fig and Walnut Bread	page 109
Roasted Pork and Autumn Vegetables	page 126

GEWÜRZTRAMINER

Jamaican Jerk Turkey Burgers with Papaya-Mango Salsa	page 72
Grilled Vegetable Salad with Tropical Vinaigrette	page 72
Hot-and-Sour Coconut Soup	page 118
Singapore Mai Fun	page 119

PINOT BLANC

Fava Bean Bruschetta	page 50

PINOT GRIS/PINOT GRIGIO

Salmon with Arugula Sauce	page 50
White Bean and Bacon Dip with Rosemary Pita Chips	page 62
Tomato, Basil, and Fresh Mozzarella Salad	page 62
Grilled Chicken with White Barbecue Sauce	page 65
Succotash Salad	page 65
Two-Potato Salad with Crème Fraîche	page 66

RIESLING

Pork Tenderloin with Nectarine-Apricot Salsa	page 97
Curried Butternut Squash Soup	page 106
Pear-Cheese Strata	page 106
Raisin-Rosemary Rye Bread	page 109
Spiced Fig and Walnut Bread	page 109
Citrus Chicken Tagine	page 131
Pork Cassoulet	page 180

SAUVIGNON BLANC

Field Salad with Snow Peas, Grapes, and Feta	page 26
Frittata with Spinach, Potatoes, and Leeks	page 26
Roasted Fig and Arugula Salad	page 78
Grilled Lemon-Bay Shrimp	page 78
Barley Risotto with Fennel and Olives	page 80
Classic Caesar Salad	page 122

VERNACCIA

Penne with Tomatoes, Olives, and Capers	page 87

ROSÉS AND REDS

BORDEAUX

Pistachio-Encrusted Rack of Lamb	page 34

CABERNET SAUVIGNON

Beef Tenderloin with Warm Vegetable Salad	page 84

CHÂTEAUNEUF-DU-PAPE

Apple Cider-Brined Turkey with Savory Herb Gravy	page 135
Herbed Bread Stuffing	page 136
Brown Sugar-Glazed Sweet Potato Wedges	page 138

CÔTES-DU-RHÔNE

Hunter's Stew	page 122

MERLOT

Beef Tenderloin with Parsnip-Mushroom Ragoût	page 149

PINOT NOIR

Turkey Sandwich with Red Pepper-Pine Nut Pesto and Caramelized Onions	page 31
Rich Mushroom Soup	page 169
Roasted Salmon and Leeks in Phyllo Packets	page 185

RIOJA

Rosemary-Grilled Lamb Chops	page 91

ROSÉ

Fennel, Orange, and Parmigiano Salad	page 44
Fisherman's Seafood Stew	page 164

SANGIOVESE

Mushroom and Parmigiano Bruschetta	page 38
Rosemary- and Pepper-Crusted Pork Tenderloin	page 38
Three-Grain Risotto with Asparagus Spears	page 40

SYRAH/SHIRAZ

Beef Stew	page 174

ZINFANDEL

Grilled Chicken with White Barbecue Sauce	page 65

Note: Side dishes are not included here unless they are recipes I think are exceptional matches with the wine. Also, I have not included the dessert wine and recipe pairings in this chart; see pages 160 and 161 for specific information about dessert wines.

spring

What sort of wine is perfect for spring?
One with freshness, liveliness, and the fleeting perfumes of
fruits and flowers. But, above all, the wine must possess that invigorating
spirit nature designed us to experience as we emerge from the
darkness of winter into the brilliant light of springtime.

—Kermit Lynch, American author and wine importer

Spring fills me with a compelling urge to cook.

Maybe it's the pure delight of walking into a market and suddenly finding tender sweet lettuces, fresh fragrant baby peas, and the earliest pencil-thin asparagus. Or maybe it's the pristine smell of the air—cool and warm at the same time—as I throw open windows that have been clamped shut for months. Or maybe—indeed, *surely* this, too—it's walking in my vineyard and seeing the very first tiny and heart-stoppingly beautiful emerald green shoots that have just emerged from the no-longer dormant vines. Spring, the most eternal of surprises, is also—for me—the most moving of the seasons. Spring always feels like a gift. And so it is that I find myself

Instinctively, I'll open a wine that's vividly fresh, clean, and crisp—a wine that tastes like the very embodiment of spring.

in the kitchen, happy to be surrounded by mountains of fresh herbs and produce. Instinctively, I'll open a wine that's vividly fresh, clean, and crisp—a wine that tastes like the very embodiment of spring. Such wines are not only inspiring to sip while cooking springtime fare, but also just feel right with spring's best dishes.

spring brunch

This simple, graceful meal exudes the freshness of spring. With it, I serve two stellar wines that make these dishes even more vividly delicious. One selection is a familiar springtime favorite; the other is a classic wine that has been a well-kept secret—till now!

menu | wine

Field Salad with Snow Peas, Grapes, and Feta

Frittata with Spinach, Potatoes, and Leeks

Lemon-Blueberry Muffins

———

Strawberry-Almond Cream Tart

Serves 6

Green vegetables are pure spring on the palate. With their snappy, almost racy freshness, they need—indeed, they *demand*—a wine that dances with clean, vibrant flavor. And if that vibrant flavor also happens to be "green" itself, well, all the better. One wine—sauvignon blanc—fits the bill exactly and it's just the ticket to open this meal. For such foods as salad, snow peas, spinach, and leeks, sauvignon blanc is a virtual soul mate, a lime laser of a wine that mirrors any sort of greenness. It's also one of the best all-around wines for salty, dry, tangy cheeses, such as feta, as well as the perfect choice whenever a dish is herbal or citrusy. The field salad and frittata—even the muffins—are, quite frankly, tailor-made for sauvignon blanc.

Finding a terrific sauvignon blanc is easy. Delicious sauvignons are made everywhere from the Napa Valley to Sancerre (France), from New Zealand to South Africa. For the savory dishes featured here, I've chosen one of my favorites: **St. Supéry Sauvignon Blanc** ($$), from the Napa Valley.

The first time I made this Strawberry-Almond Cream Tart, I thought it was scrumptious. The second time, I drank a glass of muscat de Beaumes-de-Venise alongside—and it was heaven. Muscat de Beaumes-de-Venise is a sweet (but not sugary), lightly fortified wine named after the village of Beaumes-de-Venise in the southern Rhône Valley of France, not far from Châteauneuf-du-Pape. Made from intensely aromatic muscat grapes, the wine is an explosion of peach, apricot, and citrus flavors. It's a deliciously fruity contrast to the tart's creamy berryness. Try **Domaine de Coyeux Muscat de Beaumes-de-Venise** ($$ for a 375-milliliter half bottle).

St. Supéry Sauvignon Blanc

Domaine de Coyeux Muscat de Beaumes-de-Venise

entertaining tip

Instead of having one big centerpiece, try decorating with a variety of small glass vases in several small arrangements on the table. Small arrangements are more conducive to conversation, since guests can still easily see each other. Use fresh blossoms or herbs from your garden or from the supermarket, but avoid highly perfumed flowers, such as lilies, because they'll overpower the aroma of the wine.

The word *sauvignon* comes from two French words—*sauvage* and *vigne*—that together mean wild (savage) vine. It makes *sauvignon blanc* a fitting name for a wine that usually has a wild streak of green flavor.

Field Salad with Snow Peas, Grapes, and Feta

The sweetness of fresh snow peas and grapes is balanced perfectly by sharp feta in this crisp green salad.

St. Supéry Sauvignon Blanc

    5   tablespoons balsamic vinegar
    5   tablespoons fresh orange juice
    2   tablespoons extravirgin olive oil
 2 ½   teaspoons sugar
    ½   teaspoon salt
    ¼   teaspoon freshly ground black pepper
    8   cups gourmet salad greens
    2   cups snow peas, trimmed and cut
        lengthwise into thin strips
    2   cups seedless red grapes, halved
    ½   cup (2 ounces) crumbled feta cheese

1. Combine first 6 ingredients in a small bowl; stir well with a whisk. Combine remaining ingredients in a large bowl. Drizzle dressing over salad; toss well. Yield: 6 servings.

CALORIES 151 (47% from fat); FAT 7.9g (sat 2.6g, mono 4.2g, poly 0.7g); PROTEIN 4.3g; CARB 18.6g; FIBER 3.0g; CHOL 11mg; IRON 2.0mg; SODIUM 354mg; CALC 123mg

Frittata with Spinach, Potatoes, and Leeks

Of all egg dishes, frittatas are the most wine-friendly, thanks to their slightly crusty, slightly caramelized exterior as well as the fact that the ratio of egg to filling is low.

St. Supéry Sauvignon Blanc

    1   teaspoon butter
    2   cups thinly sliced leek (about 2 large)
    1   (10-ounce) package fresh spinach
    ⅓   cup fat-free milk
    2   tablespoons finely chopped fresh basil
    ½   teaspoon salt
    ¼   teaspoon black pepper
    4   large eggs
    4   large egg whites
    2   cups cooked, peeled red potato (about
        ¾ pound)
 Cooking spray
 1 ½ tablespoons dry breadcrumbs
    ½   cup (2 ounces) shredded provolone
        cheese

1. Preheat oven to 350°.
2. Melt butter in a Dutch oven over medium heat. Add leek; sauté 4 minutes. Add spinach; sauté 2 minutes or until spinach wilts. Place mixture in a colander, pressing until barely moist.
3. Combine milk, basil, salt, pepper, eggs, and egg whites; stir well with a whisk. Add leek mixture and potato. Pour into a 10-inch round ceramic baking dish or pie plate coated with cooking spray. Sprinkle with breadcrumbs, and top with cheese. Bake at 350° for 25 minutes or until center is set.
4. Preheat broiler.
5. Broil frittata 4 minutes or until golden brown. Cut into wedges. Yield: 6 servings (serving size: 1 wedge).

CALORIES 185 (35% from fat); FAT 7.1g (sat 3.0g, mono 1.5g, poly 0.6g); PROTEIN 12.5g; CARB 18.9g; FIBER 2.8g; CHOL 150mg; IRON 3.0mg; SODIUM 429mg; CALC 176mg

Frittata with Spinach, Potatoes, and Leeks;
Field Salad with Snow Peas, Grapes, and Feta

Lemon-Blueberry Muffins

The sweet citrus glaze drizzled over the muffins complements the flavor of the berries.

St. Supéry Sauvignon Blanc

  2 cups all-purpose flour
  ½ cup granulated sugar
  1 teaspoon baking powder
  ½ teaspoon baking soda
  ½ teaspoon salt
  ⅛ teaspoon ground nutmeg
  ¼ cup butter
1¼ cups low-fat buttermilk
  1 tablespoon grated lemon rind
  1 large egg
  1 cup blueberries
    Cooking spray
  ½ cup powdered sugar
  1 tablespoon fresh lemon juice

1. Preheat oven to 400°.
2. Lightly spoon flour into dry measuring cups; level with a knife. Combine flour and next 5 ingredients in a medium bowl; cut in butter with a pastry blender or 2 knives until mixture resembles coarse meal.
3. Combine buttermilk, rind, and egg; stir well with a whisk. Add to flour mixture; stir just until moist. Gently fold in blueberries.
4. Spoon batter into 12 muffin cups coated with cooking spray. Bake at 400° for 20 minutes or until the muffins spring back when lightly touched. Remove muffins from pans immediately, and place on a wire rack to cool.
5. Combine powdered sugar and lemon juice in a small bowl. Drizzle glaze evenly over cooled muffins. Yield: 1 dozen (serving size: 1 muffin).

CALORIES 187 (23% from fat); FAT 4.8g (sat 2.7g, mono 1.4g, poly 0.3g); PROTEIN 3.7g; CARB 32.6g; FIBER 1.0g; CHOL 30mg; IRON 1.1mg; SODIUM 264mg; CALC 59mg

Strawberry-Almond Cream Tart

Nothing says spring like juicy fresh strawberries, especially when they're topping a tender tart. You'll have extra glaze—try it on ice cream or pound cake.

Domaine de Coyeux Muscat de Beaumes-de-Venise

CRUST:
36 honey graham crackers (about 9 sheets)
  2 tablespoons sugar
  2 tablespoons butter, melted
  4 teaspoons water
    Cooking spray

FILLING:
  ⅔ cup light cream cheese
  ¼ cup sugar
  ½ teaspoon vanilla extract
  ¼ teaspoon almond extract

TOPPING:
  6 cups small fresh strawberries, divided
  ⅔ cup sugar
  1 tablespoon cornstarch
  1 tablespoon fresh lemon juice
  2 tablespoons sliced almonds, toasted

1. Preheat oven to 350°.
2. To prepare crust, place crackers in a food processor; process until crumbly. Add 2 tablespoons sugar, butter, and water; pulse just until moist. Place mixture in a 9-inch round removable-bottom tart pan coated with cooking spray, pressing into bottom and up sides of pan to ¾ inch. Bake at 350° for 10 minutes or until lightly browned. Cool completely on a wire rack.
3. To prepare filling, combine cream cheese, ¼ cup sugar, and extracts in a medium bowl; stir until smooth. Spread mixture evenly over bottom of tart shell.
4. To prepare topping, place 2 cups strawberries in food processor; process until pureed. Combine strawberry puree, ⅔ cup sugar, and cornstarch in a small saucepan over medium heat, stirring with a whisk. Bring to a boil, stirring constantly. Reduce

heat to low; cook 1 minute. Remove glaze from heat, and cool to room temperature, stirring occasionally.
5. Combine 4 cups strawberries and juice; toss to coat. Arrange berries, bottoms up, in a circular pattern over filling. Spoon half of glaze evenly over berries (reserve remaining glaze for another use). Sprinkle nuts around edge. Cover and chill 3 hours. Yield: 10 servings.
NOTE: You can use either an 8 x 12-inch rectangular pan or a 9-inch round tart pan. The recipe also works with a 9-inch springform pan or a 10-inch pie plate.

CALORIES 289 (28% from fat); FAT 8.9g (sat 4.2g, mono 1.7g, poly 0.5g); PROTEIN 4.5g; CARB 48.7g; FIBER 3.0g; CHOL 15mg; IRON 1.3mg; SODIUM 242mg; CALC 59mg

about the wine

Muscat de Beaumes-de-Venise (the wine selected to go with the Strawberry-Almond Cream Tart) is a fortified sweet wine (known as *vin doux naturel* in French), meaning that a small amount of neutral grape spirits are added to it. This gives the wine extra punch, making its already dramatic fruit flavors that much bolder.

Strawberry-Almond Cream Tart

patio lunch italian-style

Of all the extraordinary wine-and-food marriages, one of the most traditional is simply bringing together a glass of red wine and a hunk of country bread. Drizzle the bread with extravirgin olive oil, and you've got what Italians call *Santa Trinità Mediterranea* (Mediterranean Holy Trinity). If all three—the wine, the bread, the oil—are of the very best quality, this humble combination becomes a meal in itself.

menu | wine

Turkey Sandwich with Red Pepper-Pine Nut Pesto and Caramelized Onions

Red grapes

Store-bought almond biscotti

Serves 4

What goes with turkey? That's a question I'm asked all the time. But there *isn't* a perfect wine for turkey. Everything depends on how the turkey is seasoned or how it's accompanied. Here, the basil, red bell peppers, onions, watercress, and cheese are all as important as the turkey itself. When such savory flavors are (literally) sandwiched together, I love to complement them with pinot noir. Pinot noir is admittedly pricey, but a really good bottle, such as **Cristom "Jessie Vineyard" Pinot Noir** ($$$$), from the Willamette Valley of Oregon, has an earthy suppleness that beautifully underscores the mellow meatiness of the turkey. Pinot is also one of the best red wine choices when pesto and watercress are in the picture, since pinot itself often exudes a faintly herbal, dried leaf character. Top pinots also possess a "sweet spot," a core of ripeness that mirrors the savory-sweetness of the caramelized onions. And, finally, compared with other red wines, pinot noir is silky and sleek, making it a fascinating counterpoint to such cheeses as fontina.

OK, here's an admission: My idea of the perfect dessert is a plateful of cookies. And of all the cookies I adore, I have a special fondness for biscotti. They're the only cookies I know of that, from the minute of their invention, have always had an indispensable wine partner—and that wine is Tuscan *vin santo* (holy wine). In Italy, it's traditional (if not obligatory) to dunk a biscotto in a glass of vin santo before taking a bite of the cookie. This softens the dry crunch of the cookie and provides a counterpoint to the lusciousness of the wine. Vin santo has a lively, rustic honey-and-roasted almond flavor—and the color can be unreal, from light mahogany to iridescent amber. Buy the best vin santo you can afford; cheap examples taste just that. One of my favorites is **Isole e Olena Vin Santo Del Chianti Classico** ($$$$).

Cristom "Jessie Vineyard" Pinot Noir

Isole e Olena Vin Santo Del Chianti Classico

Turkey Sandwich with Red Pepper-Pine Nut Pesto and Caramelized Onions

Ciabatta (chee-a-BAH-ta) is ideal for a rustic Italian-style sandwich because it's crunchy on the outside and soft on the inside. If you can't find a loaf of ciabatta at your local bakery, focaccia is a good substitute.

Cristom "Jessie Vineyard" Pinot Noir

¼ cup chopped fresh basil
2 tablespoons grated fresh Parmigiano-Reggiano cheese
1 tablespoon pine nuts, toasted
2 garlic cloves, halved
1 (7-ounce) bottle roasted red bell peppers, drained
2 teaspoons extravirgin olive oil
2 cups vertically sliced onion
2 teaspoons sugar
1 (8-ounce) loaf ciabatta
12 (1-ounce) slices cooked turkey breast
2 (1-ounce) slices fontina cheese
2 cups trimmed watercress or arugula

1. Place first 5 ingredients in a blender; process until smooth.

2. Heat oil in a large nonstick skillet over medium-high heat. Add onion and sugar; cook 8 minutes or until onion is browned, stirring occasionally.

3. Cut bread loaf in half horizontally; spread pepper mixture evenly over cut sides of bread. Layer turkey, fontina cheese, onion, and watercress over bottom half of loaf; top with remaining loaf half. Cut loaf into 4 pieces. Serve immediately. Yield: 4 servings (serving size: ¼ of loaf).

CALORIES 416 (25% from fat); FAT 11.5g (sat 4.4g, mono 4.5g, poly 1.6g); PROTEIN 37.5g; CARB 39.9g; FIBER 3.6g; CHOL 90mg; IRON 3.4mg; SODIUM 572mg; CALC 217mg

about the wine

Biscotti (the dessert I recommend to pair with the sandwich) and vin santo are traditional partners. To make vin santo, bunches of trebbiano and malvasia grapes are harvested and then hung up on hooks in an airy, dry attic or other room. Over the course of three to six months, the grapes shrivel as the water in them evaporates, leaving only concentrated sugar behind. After the grapes are pressed, the juice is sealed inside chestnut and oak casks, where it is allowed to ferment and mature for years. Many Tuscan families make their own vin santo and offer it to guests as a special welcome. Vin santo should be served at coolish room temperature.

Wine to me is passion. It's family and friends. It's warmth of heart and generosity of spirit.

—Robert Mondavi, winemaker

Pistachio-Encrusted Rack of Lamb

elegant seasonal dinner

Throughout the Mediterranean, the affinity between lamb and wine is centuries old. Together, they are a celebration and symbol of spring. Therefore, with this menu, I love to serve one of the great wines of France: a fine red Bordeaux.

menu | wine

Pistachio-Encrusted Rack of Lamb

New Potatoes with Balsamic-Shallot Butter

Steamed sugar snap peas

Whole-grain rolls

Serves 4

French food-and-wine matches are often exciting, but for me none is more purely satisfying than roasted lamb and red Bordeaux. Like so many European pairings, the precedent for this duo was practical: Before the mid-1900s, sheep from the countryside in Bordeaux were often left to graze in the famous vineyards over the winter. Because the wild grasses and herbs that grew between the rows had especially delicious flavor, so did the lamb. While sheep no longer graze in these vineyards, a wonderful synergy remains between lamb's meaty, rich, wild flavor and the slightly herbal, deep cassis (black currant) flavors of red Bordeaux.

Château Gruaud Larose

Bordeaux is the largest fine wine region in the world. More than seven hundred million bottles are produced there each year, so there's a lot of Bordeaux from which to choose. Frankly, though, some of it is very simple stuff. For this lamb dish, however, a truly fine Bordeaux is in order—and there's no way around it, it will be expensive. I've chosen one of my favorites: **Château Gruaud Larose** ($$$$), from St.-Julien. The wine's soaring majestic structure, plush texture, and aromas and flavors of cedar, spices, cassis, baked plums, and dark cocoa are all perfectly calibrated for succulent lamb. Moreover, Bordeaux such as this often have a faint hint of mint, as well as something that smells tantalizingly like fine vanilla-scented pipe tobacco. Both characteristics shine when the lamb is seasoned with herbs and nuts, as this lamb dish is. Red Bordeaux wines are always blends of merlot and cabernet sauvignon (either one can be in the lead) with cabernet franc plus small amounts of malbec and petit verdot. When grown in a top Bordeaux vineyard, merlot and cabernet sauvignon are like racehorses: powerful, intense, and thrilling.

about the wine

The Bordeaux region is one of the largest vineyard areas on the globe, roughly seven times the size of California's Napa Valley. When choosing a fine Bordeaux wine, make sure it's from one of the top six areas within Bordeaux (known as communes): Margaux, St.-Julien, Pauillac, St.-Estèphe, St.-Emilion, and Pomerol.

Fine Bordeaux reds are primarily based on merlot, cabernet sauvignon, and usually a smaller amount of cabernet franc. All three varieties have a lot of tannin, which is a compound in grape skins and seeds that gives the final wine structure and ageability. Structure is hard to describe, but it's the sense that the wine has a framework (the French call this the wine's "skeleton"). Ageability means the wine is built to last. Top Bordeaux can easily be cellared for a decade or more. So besides being delicious to drink now, a bottle of top Bordeaux is always a great gift.

Pistachio-Encrusted Rack of Lamb

This striking dish is ultrasimple to make. You can prepare the mustard mixture early in the day. The breadcrumb mixture (minus the lemon juice) can also be prepared ahead; just remember to add the juice before patting the pistachio crust onto the lamb.

Château Gruaud Larose (Bordeaux)

  1 (1.5-ounce) slice day-old white bread
2½ tablespoons finely chopped pistachios
  ½ teaspoon grated lemon rind
  1 tablespoon finely chopped parsley
  2 tablespoons lemon juice
  ½ teaspoon salt, divided
  2 tablespoons finely chopped fresh chives
  2 tablespoons finely chopped fresh mint
  1 tablespoon Dijon mustard
  1 garlic clove, minced
  1 (1½-pound) French-cut racks of lamb (8 ribs), trimmed
Cooking spray
Mint sprigs (optional)

1. Preheat oven to 425°.
2. Place bread in a food processor; pulse 10 times or until coarse crumbs form to measure about ⅔ cup.
3. Combine breadcrumbs, nuts, rind, parsley, juice, and ¼ teaspoon salt in a small bowl.
4. Combine chives, mint, mustard, and garlic in a small bowl.
5. Sprinkle lamb with ¼ teaspoon salt. Heat a large nonstick skillet coated with cooking spray over medium-high heat. Add lamb rack; cook 2 minutes on each side or until browned. Spread mustard mixture evenly over meaty portion of lamb rack. Carefully pat breadcrumb mixture into mustard mixture.
6. Place lamb on a broiler pan coated with cooking spray. Bake at 425° for 35 minutes or until meat thermometer registers 145° (medium-rare) to 160° (medium). Place lamb on a platter; cover with foil. Let stand 10 minutes before serving (temperature will increase 5° upon standing). Cut rack into 4 pieces (2 ribs per piece). Garnish with mint sprigs, if desired. Yield: 4 servings (serving size: 1 piece [2 ribs]).

CALORIES 206 (47% from fat); FAT 10.8g (sat 3.1g, mono 4.6g, poly 1.5g); PROTEIN 18.5g; CARB 8.5g; FIBER 0.9g; CHOL 52mg; IRON 2.1mg; SODIUM 530mg; CALC 37mg

New Potatoes with Balsamic-Shallot Butter

The balsamic-butter mixture is deep brown and tastes sweet and rich. You can make it ahead, chill, and then toss with the potatoes just before serving.

Château Gruaud Larose (Bordeaux)

  ⅓ cup balsamic vinegar
2½ tablespoons butter, softened
1½ tablespoons finely chopped shallots
  1 teaspoon chopped fresh thyme
  ¼ teaspoon salt, divided
Dash of freshly ground black pepper
  2 pounds small red potatoes
  1 tablespoon finely chopped parsley

1. Bring vinegar to a boil in a small saucepan; reduce heat, and simmer until reduced to 1 tablespoon (about 5 minutes). Place in a medium bowl, and cool completely. Add butter, chopped shallots, thyme, ⅛ teaspoon salt, and black pepper; stir well to combine.
2. Place potatoes in a saucepan; cover with water. Bring to a boil, reduce heat, and simmer 20 minutes or until tender. Drain. Cut potatoes in half; place in a large bowl. Sprinkle with ⅛ teaspoon salt, Add butter mixture and parsley; toss gently to coat. Serve immediately. Yield: 4 servings (serving size: 1¼ cups).

CALORIES 242 (28% from fat); FAT 7.5g (sat 3.6g, mono 2.9g, poly 0.4g); PROTEIN 4.5g; CARB 39.9g; FIBER 3.9g; CHOL 19mg; IRON 2.0mg; SODIUM 218mg; CALC 34mg

New Potatoes with
Balsamic-Shallot Butter

Three-Grain Risotto with Asparagus Spears,
Rosemary- and Pepper-Crusted Pork Tenderloin

dinner alfresco

The first warm breezes of spring are our invitation to dine outdoors. And there's no better way to begin—*and* end—the meal than with the Italian alfresco classics bruschetta and granita. Bruschetta always seems to taste just a bit better when served in the backyard, and granita is the quintessence of spring flavor.

menu | wine

menu

Mushroom and Parmigiano Bruschetta

Rosemary- and Pepper-Crusted Pork Tenderloin

Three-Grain Risotto with Asparagus Spears

Green salad

Fresh Strawberry Granita

Serves 4

wine

The first time I tried bruschetta I was standing in a backyard garden in Italy and the smell of the springtime air plus the crunch of the savory bruschetta was so simple—yet so perfect—that I'll never forget the experience. We drank the traditional wine: Chianti Classico from Tuscany, which is made primarily from sangiovese grapes. Light bodied enough to begin the meal, Chianti Classico has an earthy, woodsy, Bing cherry, dried rose petal character that's a wonderful complement to the earthy mushrooms and the nutty sweetness of the Parmigiano-Reggiano. One of my favorites is **Querciabella Chianti Classico** ($$$).

With Chianti Classico as the perfect opener, the stage is set for another Tuscan red—Brunello di Montalcino—to accompany the pork. Considered Chianti's "big brother," brunello is also made from sangiovese grapes, but it's significantly more powerful and fuller bodied than Chianti. With its mesmerizing aromas—evocative of roasted espresso beans, dark chocolate, black peppercorns, tar, and moist black soil—brunello is traditionally served with wild boar ragoût and other super-meaty meat dishes. Here, the savory richness of the pork tenderloin, the wild herb spiciness of the rosemary and black pepper, and the nuttiness of the three-grain risotto are all great foils for such a majestic brunello as **Col d'Orcia Brunello di Montalcino** ($$$$). (If Brunello di Montalcino is too pricey, consider Rosso di Montalcino, a younger, lighter version that is aged less in oak and can be half the cost.)

Fresh Strawberry Granita is an explosion of sweet wild berryness and tastes devastatingly good with a light-bodied dessert wine that won't overwhelm its delicacy. My top choice is an outrageously fruity, racy moscato, such as **Robert Pecota Moscato d'Andrea** ($ for a 375-milliliter half bottle), from California's Napa Valley.

Querciabella Chianti Classico

Col d'Orcia Brunello di Montalcino

Robert Pecota Moscato d'Andrea

Mushroom and
Parmigiano Bruschetta

Mushroom and Parmigiano Bruschetta

The name *bruschetta* (broo-SKEH-tah) comes from the Italian word meaning "to roast over coals" and is a handheld appetizer featuring toasted bread and a savory topping. You can use any combination of fresh mushrooms in this recipe, and while shaved Parmigiano-Reggiano cheese looks handsome, you can also grate the cheese and stir it into the mushroom mixture.

Querciabella Chianti Classico

- ½ cup chopped seeded plum tomato
- 2 tablespoons Sherry vinegar
- 1 teaspoon capers
- ½ teaspoon sugar
- ¼ teaspoon crushed red pepper
- ⅛ teaspoon salt
- 10 thinly sliced basil leaves
- 2 teaspoons butter
- ⅓ cup sliced cremini mushrooms
- ⅓ cup sliced shiitake mushroom caps
- ⅓ cup sliced baby portobello mushroom caps
- ¼ cup chopped green onions
- 1 garlic clove, minced
- 8 (½-inch-thick) slices diagonally cut French bread baguette, toasted
- ¼ cup (1 ounce) shaved Parmigiano-Reggiano cheese

1. Combine first 7 ingredients in a medium bowl; set aside.

2. Melt butter in a medium nonstick skillet over medium heat. Add mushrooms, onions, and garlic; cook 5 minutes or until tender, stirring frequently. Add mushroom mixture to tomato mixture; toss well to combine.

3. Spoon about 1 tablespoon mushroom mixture onto each bread slice. Sprinkle evenly with cheese. Serve immediately. Yield: 4 servings (serving size: 2 topped bruschetta).

CALORIES 145 (30% from fat); FAT 4.8g (sat 2.6g, mono 1.5g, poly 0.4g); PROTEIN 6.1g; CARB 19.5g; FIBER 1.8g; CHOL 10mg; IRON 1.3mg; SODIUM 420mg; CALC 114mg

Rosemary- and Pepper-Crusted Pork Tenderloin

Crush the fennel seeds with a mortar and pestle; or place the seeds in a zip-top plastic bag, and crush with a rolling pin.

Col d'Orcia Brunello di Montalcino

- 2 teaspoons cracked black pepper
- 1 teaspoon dried rosemary, crushed
- ½ teaspoon kosher salt
- ½ teaspoon fennel seeds, crushed
- ½ teaspoon dry mustard
- 1 (1-pound) pork tenderloin, trimmed
  Cooking spray
- 2 tablespoons chopped fresh flat-leaf parsley

1. Preheat oven to 425°.

2. Combine first 5 ingredients; rub over pork. Place pork in a shallow roasting pan coated with cooking spray. Bake at 425° for 30 minutes or until a thermometer registers 160° (slightly pink). Let stand 5 minutes; cut into thin slices. Sprinkle with parsley. Yield: 4 servings (serving size: 3 ounces).

CALORIES 158 (31% from fat); FAT 5.4g (sat 1.8g, mono 2.2g, poly 0.5g); PROTEIN 24.7g; CARB 1.3g; FIBER 0.6g; CHOL 75mg; IRON 1.8mg; SODIUM 289mg; CALC 23mg

> ## With inimitable fragrance and soft fire ... wine is bottled poetry.
>
> —Robert Louis Stevenson, Scottish author

about the wine

When you're selecting a Chianti, keep in mind that there are three different types. There's regular Chianti, and then there's Chianti Classico and Chianti Classico Riserva. While Classico and Classico Riserva cost a little more than regular Chianti, I recommend you trade up to them because they deliver so much more flavor.

Chianti: The least expensive type, simple Chiantis can be made anywhere in the large Chianti zone that spans roughly half the land of Tuscany. Often a blend of sangiovese with canaiolo, these wines are generally aged at least five months but usually less than one year.

Chianti Classico: Moderately expensive, Chianti Classicos come from a far smaller zone—the original, or "classico," hilly area between Florence and Siena, known for rich wines. Chianti Classicos are often 100 percent sangiovese and are usually aged at least one year.

Chianti Classico Riserva: The most expensive type of Chianti, Chianti Classico Riserva must be aged a minimum of two years, dating from the first day of January following the harvest. For at least three months of that time, the wine must age in bottles rather than barrels. Chianti Classico Riservas are also often 100 percent sangiovese and are usually made only in years with top harvests.

good cook tip

Here is the most wine-friendly way to prepare asparagus spears: Grill them. Grilling caramelizes the starches in the asparagus, bringing out a touch of sweetness. At the same time, grilling causes the asparagus to take on a smoky, charred flavor that's a fascinating juxtaposition to the flavors of many wines.

To grill asparagus expertly, lightly brush spears with olive oil. Place spears on a grill rack coated with cooking spray; grill over a medium-hot fire, turning frequently, 4 to 6 minutes or until spears begin to soften, brown, and crisp.

Three-Grain Risotto with Asparagus Spears

Instead of featuring just short-grain rice, this risotto has a variety of heart-healthy grains—rice, barley, and quinoa—that gives it contrasting textures: creaminess from the rice, chewiness from the barley, and crunchiness from the quinoa.

Col d'Orcia Brunello di Montalcino

- 1/8 teaspoon saffron threads, crushed
- 1 (14-ounce) can fat-free, less-sodium chicken broth
- 1 tablespoon olive oil
- 1/4 cup finely chopped shallots (about 2 medium)
- 1/2 cup uncooked Arborio or other short-grain rice
- 1/2 cup uncooked quick-cooking barley
- 1/4 cup uncooked quinoa
- 1/2 cup dry white wine
- 1 cup water
- 1 cup (4 ounces) shredded part-skim mozzarella cheese
- 2/3 cup 1% low-fat milk
- 2 teaspoons fresh lemon juice
- 1/2 teaspoon salt
- 1/2 teaspoon freshly ground black pepper
- 12 asparagus spears, grilled
- 1 tablespoon pine nuts, toasted

1. Bring saffron and broth to a simmer in a small saucepan (do not boil). Keep warm over low heat.

2. Heat oil in a large saucepan over medium-high heat. Add shallots; sauté 3 minutes. Add rice, barley, and quinoa; sauté 2 minutes. Add wine; cook 2 minutes or until liquid is nearly absorbed. Stir in 1 cup water; cook 5 minutes or until liquid is nearly absorbed, stirring constantly. Add broth mixture, 1/2 cup at a time, stirring constantly until each portion of broth mixture is absorbed before adding the next (about 25 minutes total).

3. Remove from heat; stir in cheese and next 4 ingredients. Top with asparagus spears, and sprinkle with pine nuts. Yield: 4 servings (serving size: about 1 cup risotto, 3 asparagus spears, and about 1 teaspoon pine nuts).

CALORIES 393 (24% from fat); FAT 10.5g (sat 3.9g, mono 4.5g, poly 1.4g); PROTEIN 17.3g; CARB 57.3g; FIBER 6.3g; CHOL 18mg; IRON 2.9mg; SODIUM 638mg; CALC 275mg

Fresh Strawberry Granita

This refreshing frozen dessert doesn't require an ice-cream maker—just freeze the mixture in a pan, and then scrape with a fork.

Robert Pecota Moscato d'Andrea

- 1/2 cup sugar
- 1/2 cup warm water
- 3 cups sliced strawberries
- 2 tablespoons fresh lemon juice
- Lemon zest (optional)

1. Combine sugar and water in a blender; process until sugar dissolves. Add strawberries and juice; process until smooth. Pour mixture into an 8-inch square baking dish. Cover and freeze 3 hours; stir well. Cover and freeze 5 hours or overnight.

2. Remove mixture from freezer; let stand at room temperature 10 minutes. Scrape entire mixture with a fork until fluffy. Top each serving with lemon zest, if desired. Yield: 4 servings (serving size: 1 cup).

CALORIES 136 (3% from fat); FAT 0.5g (sat 0g, mono 0.1g, poly 0.2g); PROTEIN 0.8g; CARB 34.4g; FIBER 2.9g; CHOL 0mg; IRON 0.5mg; SODIUM 2mg; CALC 18mg

Fresh Strawberry Granita

salad days

The right wines with the right foods create a special sort of magic—and this casual meal is the perfect example. These combinations are so amazing that the foods and wines possess an almost mind-boggling deliciousness when served together. A classic case of one plus one equaling three.

menu | wine

Fennel, Orange, and Parmigiano Salad

Shrimp and White Bean Salad over Watercress

Raspberry-Almond Muffins

Sour Cream Pound Cake

Serves 12

For all its utter simplicity, Fennel, Orange, and Parmigiano Salad packs a real punch of flavor. I love to serve it with a dry rosé, such as **Red Bicyclette Rosé** ($) from Vin de Pays d'Oc in southern France. True rosé wines are much nicer (and drier!) than soft, slightly sweetish blush wines, such as most white zinfandels. This rosé has charming flavors reminiscent of wild strawberries, spiced raspberries, and citrus. It's the perfect contrast to the herbalness of the fennel, the citrusy tang of the oranges, and the salty-sweet nuttiness of the Parmigiano. Plus, dry rosés are some of the best wines in the world for any dish seasoned with garlic.

Some of the most luscious shrimp in the world are caught off the coasts of Spain, and shrimp dishes are extraordinary with Spanish wines. This is especially true of albariño—a racy white from the Rias-Baixas wine region in the northwestern Spanish province of Galicia. **Nora Albariño** ($), for example, is crisp and vivacious, with hints of peaches, almonds, citrus, and spice. It complements the shrimp and peppery watercress, while contrasting beautifully with the richness of the white beans and avocado oil. As an added boon, the hint of almondy flavor in the albariño picks up on the almondy note in the muffins.

And, finally, an irresistible wine for an irresistible dessert. One of the most exciting wines to serve with a buttery, vanilla pound cake is ice wine (or as it is spelled in Europe, *eiswein*). It's expensive, to be sure, but also devastatingly good—and sensational with pound cake. Try **Inniskillin Riesling Ice Wine** ($$$$$), from the Niagara Peninsula. (For more information on ice wine, see page 47.)

Red Bicyclette Rosé

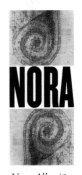

Nora Albariño

*Inniskillin
Riesling Ice Wine*

about the wine

A truly great rosé combines the best attributes of red and white wines. Because rosés are snappy and boldly fruity, they complement many Mediterranean-style dishes seasoned with olive oil, garlic, herbs, and spices. The flavor of many wines would disappear in the presence of these dramatic ingredients, but that's not the case with rosés. Rosés are best served well chilled.

Fennel, Orange, and Parmigiano Salad

If possible, use a mandoline to cut the fennel into paper-thin slices. If you don't have one of these slicers, use a very sharp knife and slice as thinly as you can.

Red Bicyclette Rosé

2	teaspoons grated orange rind
6	tablespoons fresh orange juice
2	tablespoons balsamic vinegar
2	tablespoons honey
1	tablespoon extravirgin olive oil
½	teaspoon salt
¼	teaspoon freshly ground black pepper
2	garlic cloves, minced
6	cups very thinly sliced fennel bulb (about 3 small bulbs)
6	cups torn Bibb lettuce
2½	cups orange sections
1	cup loosely packed fresh flat-leaf parsley leaves
¾	cup (3 ounces) shaved Parmigiano-Reggiano cheese

1. To prepare vinaigrette, combine first 8 ingredients in a small bowl, stirring with a whisk.

2. To prepare salad, combine fennel, lettuce, orange sections, parsley, and Parmigiano-Reggiano cheese in a large bowl; toss well. Drizzle with vinaigrette; toss gently to combine. Yield: 12 servings (serving size: 1 cup).

NOTE: You can use a domestic Parmesan cheese in this salad, but I prefer the distinctive, complex flavor of Parmigiano-Reggiano. It's worth the price. Look for the words *Parmigiano-Reggiano* imprinted on the rind of the cheese. Without this rind, it's not Parmigiano-Reggiano.

CALORIES 95 (30% from fat); FAT 3.2g (sat 1.3g, mono 1.4g, poly 0.2g); PROTEIN 4.3g; CARB 13.9g; FIBER 3.4g; CHOL 5mg; IRON 1.2mg; SODIUM 247mg; CALC 147mg

Shrimp and White Bean Salad over Watercress

Avocado oil adds a rich, buttery dimension to this hearty shrimp and bean salad. If you can't find watercress, substitute baby spinach leaves.

Nora Albariño

2½ pounds large shrimp, peeled and deveined
¾ teaspoon salt, divided
½ teaspoon freshly ground black pepper, divided
Cooking spray
2 (15-ounce) cans cannellini beans, rinsed and drained
¼ cup avocado oil or extravirgin olive oil
2 tablespoons fresh lemon juice
6 cups trimmed watercress (about 3 bunches)
3 tablespoons chopped fresh chives
Lemon wedges (optional)

1. Prepare grill.
2. Thread shrimp onto 12-inch skewers; sprinkle with ¼ teaspoon salt and ¼ teaspoon pepper. Place skewers on a grill rack coated with cooking spray; grill 3 minutes on each side or until done. Cool completely; remove shrimp from skewers. Place shrimp and beans in a large bowl; toss gently to combine.
3. Combine oil and lemon juice, stirring with a whisk; stir in ½ teaspoon salt and ¼ teaspoon pepper. Drizzle dressing over shrimp mixture; toss gently to combine.
4. Arrange watercress on a large platter, and top with shrimp mixture. Sprinkle evenly with chives. Serve with lemon wedges, if desired. Yield: 12 servings (serving size: about ¾ cup).

CALORIES 190 (30% from fat); FAT 6.4g (sat 0.9g, mono 3.6g, poly 1.3g); PROTEIN 22.0g; CARB 9.9g; FIBER 2.5g; CHOL 144mg; IRON 3.2mg; SODIUM 421mg; CALC 90mg

Raspberry-Almond Muffins

Raspberry-Almond Muffins

Almond paste is more textured and less sweet than marzipan, but either works for this recipe.

Nora Albariño

  ½ cup granulated sugar
  ½ cup packed brown sugar
  2½ tablespoons almond paste
  ¼ cup butter, softened
  2 large eggs
  ½ cup low-fat buttermilk
  1 teaspoon vanilla extract
  1 teaspoon fresh lemon juice
  2 cups all-purpose flour
  ½ teaspoon baking powder
  ½ teaspoon baking soda
  ¼ teaspoon salt
  1½ cups fresh raspberries
     Cooking spray
  2 tablespoons turbinado sugar or
     granulated sugar

1. Preheat oven to 375°.
2. Place first 3 ingredients in a food processor, and process until well blended. Add butter, and pulse 4 to 5 times or just until combined. Add eggs, 1 at a time, pulsing 1 or 2 times after each addition. Add buttermilk, vanilla, and lemon juice; pulse until blended.
3. Lightly spoon flour into dry measuring cups; level with a knife. Combine flour, baking powder, baking soda, and salt in a large bowl, stirring with a whisk. Make a well in center of mixture. Add buttermilk mixture; stir just until moist. Gently fold in raspberries. Let batter stand 5 minutes. Spoon 1 teaspoon batter into each of 48 miniature muffin cups coated with cooking spray. Sprinkle with turbinado sugar. Bake at 375° for 10 to 12 minutes or until muffins spring back when touched lightly in center. Remove muffins from pans immediately; place on a wire rack. Yield: 4 dozen (serving size: 1 muffin).

CALORIES 56 (23% from fat); FAT 1.4g (sat 0.6g, mono 0.6g, poly 0.1g); PROTEIN 1.0g; CARB 9.8g; FIBER 0.4g; CHOL 11mg; IRON 0.4mg; SODIUM 32mg; CALC 13mg

Sour Cream Pound Cake

The perfect finale: a slice of old-fashioned pound cake, a dollop of whipped cream, and some fresh berries.

Inniskillin Riesling Ice Wine

     Cooking spray
  3 tablespoons dry breadcrumbs
  3¼ cups all-purpose flour
  ½ teaspoon baking soda
  ¼ teaspoon salt
  ¾ cup butter, softened
  2½ cups granulated sugar
  2 teaspoons vanilla extract
  3 large eggs
  ¼ cup fat-free milk, divided
  1 (8-ounce) carton low-fat sour cream
  1 cup powdered sugar

1. Preheat oven to 350°.
2. Coat a 10-inch tube pan with cooking spray; dust with breadcrumbs.
3. Lightly spoon flour into dry measuring cups; level with a knife. Combine flour, baking soda, and salt in a bowl; stir well with a whisk. Beat butter in a large bowl with a mixer at medium speed until light and fluffy. Gradually add granulated sugar and vanilla extract, beating until well blended. Add eggs, 1 at a time, beating well after each addition. Add 2 tablespoons milk; beat 30 seconds. Add flour mixture to sugar mixture alternately with sour cream, beating at low speed, beginning and ending with flour mixture.
4. Spoon batter into prepared pan. Bake at 350° for 1 hour and 10 minutes or until a wooden pick inserted in center comes out clean. Cool in pan 10 minutes on a wire rack; remove from pan. Cool completely on wire rack. Combine 2 tablespoons milk and powdered sugar. Drizzle glaze over top of cake. Yield: 18 servings (serving size: 1 slice).

CALORIES 315 (29% from fat); FAT 10.2g (sat 5.1g, mono 3.5g, poly 0.5g); PROTEIN 4.3g; CARB 52.1g; FIBER 0.6g; CHOL 62mg; IRON 1.2mg; SODIUM 112mg; CALC 36mg

wine tip

Ice wine is made in winter from grapes frozen naturally on the vine. When the grapes are pressed, the water in them remains behind as ice crystals; only the purest, most luscious, and sweetest juice trickles out, eventually to be made into wine. Ice wine is painstakingly difficult to make and, as a result, expensive. But even a small sip is an unforgettable experience.

The standard amount to pour is 2 ounces, which means that a half bottle (which is how ice wine usually comes packaged) serves six people. Be sure to serve ice wine well chilled.

spring celebration

The savory courses of this elegant meal showcase some of the most exquisite flavors of spring. To frame these pure and clean flavors, I've taken my wine inspirations from Alsace, France, which is the source of some of the greatest white wines of Europe.

menu | wine

Fava Bean Bruschetta

Salmon with Arugula Sauce

Spring Risotto

Fresh Peas with Mint

Greek Easter Bread

Chocolate Pots de Crème

Serves 8

Fava beans are one of the most sophisticated and soothing flavors of spring. Smooth, palate coating, and mildly green tasting, favas are fantastic with a wine that's precise and fresh on the one hand but echoes their creaminess and weight on the other. Such a wine is Alsace pinot blanc. Unlike pinot blancs from California, those from Alsace are rarely oaky. Instead, they're vibrant and fruit driven; at the same time, they have the body to balance a creamy bean. Lastly, pinot blanc has an affinity with tarragon—the cincher in this pairing. Try the **Trimbach Pinot Blanc** ($). It's lively and fresh, with a wisp of vanilla.

With the salmon, risotto, and peas, I love to serve an Alsace pinot gris (pinot blanc's close genetic sister). A French grape by origin, pinot gris is known as pinot grigio in Italy—but there the connection ends. Full-throttle Alsace pinot gris is the opposite of ultralight and mild pinot grigio. In fact, the powerful and concentrated character of Alsace pinot gris makes it a perfect mirror for salmon (one of the richest, moistest, and most full-flavored fish). Salmon is often a good partner for red wine, too (specifically pinot noir). But the greens that surround this salmon all flatter white wine more than red. My favorite—**Domaine Weinbach "Cuvée Ste. Catherine" Pinot Gris** ($$$$)—is one of the world's best.

A cool chocolate dessert presents a challenge when it comes to pairing with wine. Chocolate has a profound, deep bitter-sweet flavor that's accentuated when the chocolate is chilled. I love to capitalize on the natural affinity between chocolate and red berries. **Bonny Doon Vineyard Framboise** ($ for a 375-milliliter half bottle), a wine made entirely from ripe raspberries, is one of the most exuberantly, outrageously delicious things I've ever tasted. Serve it nicely chilled, just like the Chocolate Pots de Crème.

Trimbach Pinot Blanc

Domaine Weinbach "Cuvée Ste. Catherine" Pinot Gris

Bonny Doon Vineyard Framboise

about the wine

The white wines of Alsace are one of Europe's best-kept secrets, except among wine pros who know from experience how fabulous they are with food. The reason? Alsace whites possess the genuinely rare quality of being both crisp and fairly full bodied at the same time. Plus, their flavors can be outrageously concentrated. The five main white grapes of Alsace are riesling, gewürztraminer, pinot gris, pinot blanc, and muscat.

Fava Bean Bruschetta

Favas, sometimes called broad beans or horse beans, are most often used in Mediterranean foods. Here, they're flavored with tarragon and lime juice and then spooned onto toasted bread slices. If you don't need 16 appetizers, just slice the amount of bread you need and store the extra bean mixture in an airtight container in the refrigerator for up to three days.

Trimbach Pinot Blanc

2 ¼ pounds unshelled fava beans
2 tablespoons extravirgin olive oil
1 tablespoon chopped fresh tarragon
1 tablespoon fresh lime juice
¼ teaspoon salt
1 garlic clove, minced
1 (1-pound) French bread baguette, cut into 32 slices and toasted
2 ounces shaved Parmesan cheese

1. Remove tough outer skin from beans; discard pods. Cook beans in boiling water 1 minute; rinse with cold water. Drain; remove outer skins from beans. Discard skins.
2. Place beans in a food processor. Add oil and next 4 ingredients; process until almost smooth. Spread about 1½ teaspoons bean mixture over each bread slice. Arrange cheese evenly over bread slices. Yield: 16 servings (serving size: 2 bruschetta).

CALORIES 115 (28% from fat); FAT 3.6g (sat 1.0g, mono 1.9g, poly 0.4g); PROTEIN 4.4g; CARB 16.0g; FIBER 1.2g; CHOL 3mg; IRON 0.9mg; SODIUM 268mg; CALC 64mg

Salmon with Arugula Sauce

Springtime is prime time for arugula, which is a peppery and slightly pungent leafy salad green. The bread helps thicken the arugula sauce for a consistency that is similar to pesto.

Domaine Weinbach "Cuvée Ste. Catherine" Pinot Gris

SAUCE:
1 cup coarsely chopped fresh parsley
1 cup chopped arugula
⅔ cup water
½ cup chopped fresh chives
¼ cup coarsely chopped walnuts, toasted
1 tablespoon capers, drained
½ teaspoon salt
¼ teaspoon freshly ground black pepper
1 garlic clove, chopped
1 (1-ounce) slice white bread
FISH:
8 (6-ounce) salmon fillets (about 1 inch thick)
½ teaspoon salt
¼ teaspoon freshly ground black pepper
Cooking spray

1. To prepare sauce, combine first 10 ingredients in a food processor; process until smooth.
2. Preheat broiler.
3. To prepare fish, sprinkle fish with ½ teaspoon salt and ¼ teaspoon pepper. Place fish on a broiler pan coated with cooking spray; broil 10 minutes or until fish flakes easily when tested with a fork. Serve fish with arugula sauce. Yield: 8 servings (serving size: 1 fillet and 2 tablespoons arugula sauce).

CALORIES 315 (45% from fat); FAT 15.8g (sat 3.4g, mono 6.1g, poly 5.0g); PROTEIN 37.8g; CARB 3.8g; FIBER 1.2g; CHOL 87mg; IRON 1.8mg; SODIUM 437mg; CALC 53mg

Spring Risotto, Fresh Peas with Mint,
Salmon with Arugula Sauce

Greek Easter Bread

This sweet, spiced loaf is not only beautiful and delicious, but also large enough to feed a holiday crowd. Use leftovers to make French toast.

Domaine Weinbach "Cuvée Ste. Catherine" Pinot Gris

  1 teaspoon whole allspice
  1 (3-inch) cinnamon stick
  1 cup warm water (100° to 110°)
Dash of salt
Dash of sugar
  2 packages dry yeast (about 2¼ teaspoons each)
4¾ cups bread flour, divided
 ½ cup sugar
  3 tablespoons butter
  3 large eggs
  1 teaspoon salt
Cooking spray
  1 tablespoon water
  1 large egg yolk

1. Place allspice and cinnamon in a spice or coffee grinder, and process until finely ground. Set aside.

2. Combine water, dash of salt, dash of sugar, and yeast in a large bowl, stirring with a whisk. Let stand for 5 minutes. Lightly spoon flour into dry measuring cups; level with a knife. Add 1 cup flour to yeast mixture, stirring until combined. Let stand 20 minutes.

3. Place ½ cup sugar and butter in a large bowl; beat with a mixer at medium speed until light and fluffy. Add eggs, 1 at a time, beating well after each addition. Stir in allspice mixture. Add yeast mixture to butter mixture; stir with a whisk until combined. Stir in 1 teaspoon salt. Add 3½ cups flour, about 1 cup at a time, stirring until a soft dough forms. Turn dough out onto a floured surface. Knead until smooth and elastic (about 8 minutes); add enough of remaining flour, 1 tablespoon at a time, to prevent dough from sticking to hands (dough will feel tacky).

4. Place dough in a large bowl coated with cooking spray, turning to coat top. Cover and let rise in a warm place (85°), free from drafts, 1 hour or until doubled in size. (Gently press two fingers into dough. If indentation remains, dough has risen enough.)

5. Divide dough into 3 equal portions, shaping each portion into a 14-inch-long rope. Place ropes lengthwise on a baking sheet coated with cooking spray (do not stretch); pinch ends together at 1 end to seal. Braid ropes; pinch loose ends to seal. Lightly coat dough with cooking spray. Cover and let rise 45 minutes or until doubled in size.

6. Preheat oven to 350°.

7. Combine 1 tablespoon water and egg yolk, stirring with a whisk. Brush half of yolk mixture over loaf. Let stand for 5 minutes. Repeat procedure with remaining yolk mixture. Bake at 350° for 30 minutes or until loaf sounds hollow when tapped. Cool on a wire rack for 20 minutes. Yield: 20 servings (serving size: 1 slice).

CALORIES 168 (18% from fat); FAT 3.3g (sat 1.5g, mono 0.9g, poly 0.4g); PROTEIN 5.3g; CARB 29.1g; FIBER 1.1g; CHOL 47mg; IRON 1.8mg; SODIUM 150mg; CALC 13mg

good cook tip

Proofing—the process of making sure that yeast is alive—is the most crucial step in baking bread. If the yeast is dead, it can't leaven bread. Live yeast swells and foams (or activates) a few minutes after it's stirred into the warm liquid.

wine tip

Screw caps on wine bottles have become not only prevalent but also chic. With screw caps, there's no chance of cork taint, a chemical compound that can infuse any wine exposed to it with a musty, wet-cardboard, damp-basement aroma. While a so-called corked wine is not harmful, it is frustrating not to be able to drink the wine. Dozens of producers, mainly in Australia and New Zealand, have started bottling their wines with top-quality screw caps, known as Stelvin caps. Although most wine drinkers assume that bottling wines with screw caps is a cheaper alternative to cork, Stelvin caps actually cost more. But they're worth it to producers, who want to be forever rid of the specter of cork taint. Studies show that screw caps do a fantastic job preserving wines' freshness and flavors. Most Stelvin-capped wines on the market are easy-drinking whites.

Spring Risotto

Use a dry white wine, such as pinot gris, in this recipe. The pinot gris will enhance the flavor of the beans, morels, and leeks.

Domaine Weinbach "Cuvée Ste. Catherine" Pinot Gris

- 6 cups boiling water, divided
- 1 cup dried morels
- 2 pounds unshelled fava beans
- 5 cups fat-free, less-sodium chicken broth
- 1 tablespoon olive oil
- 2 cups thinly sliced leek (about 3 large)
- 2 garlic cloves, minced
- 2 cups Arborio rice
- 2 tablespoons sun-dried tomato paste
- 1 cup dry white wine
- ¾ teaspoon salt
- ½ teaspoon freshly ground black pepper
- ⅓ cup sliced green onions
- ¾ cup (3 ounces) finely grated fresh Romano cheese

1. Combine 3 cups boiling water and morels in a bowl; cover and let stand for 30 minutes. Drain mushrooms; rinse with cold water. Drain and chop.
2. Remove beans from pods; discard pods. Place beans in a medium saucepan with 3 cups boiling water; cook beans 1 minute. Rinse with cold water. Drain; remove outer skins from beans. Discard skins.
3. Bring broth to a simmer in a medium saucepan (do not boil). Keep broth warm over low heat.
4. Heat olive oil in a large saucepan over medium-high heat. Add leek and garlic; sauté 2 minutes or until leek is tender. Add rice and tomato paste; cook 2 minutes, stirring constantly. Stir in wine, salt, and pepper; cook 1½ minutes or until liquid is absorbed. Stir in 1 cup broth; cook about 2½ minutes or until the liquid is nearly absorbed, stirring constantly. Add remaining broth, 1 cup at a time, stirring constantly until each portion of broth is absorbed before adding the next (about 20 minutes total). Stir in morels and beans; cook for 30 seconds or until thoroughly heated. Stir in green onions. Sprinkle each serving with cheese. Yield: 8 servings (serving size: 1 cup risotto and 1½ tablespoons cheese).

CALORIES 238 (22% from fat); FAT 5.9g (sat 2.2g, mono 2.9g, poly 0.4g); PROTEIN 9.9g; CARB 29.7g; FIBER 1.6g; CHOL 11mg; IRON 2.6mg; SODIUM 648mg; CALC 135mg

Fresh Peas with Mint

When you're selecting peas, look for pods that are plump, firm, and bright green. Store peas in a plastic bag in the refrigerator for up to one day, and shell just before cooking.

Domaine Weinbach "Cuvée Ste. Catherine" Pinot Gris

- 1 tablespoon butter
- 1 cup sliced green onions
- 2 garlic cloves, minced
- 4 cups shelled green peas (about 3½ pounds unshelled)
- 1 cup water
- 1 cup fat-free, less-sodium chicken broth
- 1 tablespoon honey
- ½ teaspoon salt
- ¼ cup chopped fresh mint

1. Melt butter in a medium saucepan over medium-high heat. Add onions and garlic; sauté 1 minute. Add peas, water, broth, honey, and salt; bring to a boil. Reduce heat, and simmer 12 minutes or until peas are tender. Remove from heat; stir in mint. Serve with a slotted spoon. Yield: 8 servings (serving size: ½ cup).

CALORIES 89 (17% from fat); FAT 1.7g (sat 1.0g, mono 0.4g, poly 0.2g); PROTEIN 4.4g; CARB 14.2g; FIBER 4.3g; CHOL 4mg; IRON 1.1mg; SODIUM 220mg; CALC 22mg

Chocolate Pots de Crème

Pots de crème are creamy custards served in tiny cups. Make this dessert the night before, and chill until you're ready to serve.

Bonny Doon Vineyard Framboise

2½ cups fat-free milk
¾ cup sugar
¼ cup unsweetened cocoa
⅛ teaspoon salt
1 teaspoon vanilla extract
4 ounces semisweet or bittersweet chocolate, chopped
2 large eggs, lightly beaten
Shaved semisweet or bittersweet chocolate (optional)

1. Preheat oven to 350°.

2. Combine milk, sugar, cocoa, and salt in a medium saucepan over medium heat. Cook until sugar dissolves, stirring occasionally (about 3 minutes). Add vanilla and chopped chocolate; stir until chocolate melts.

3. Gradually add ¼ cup hot milk mixture to beaten eggs, stirring constantly with a whisk. Add egg mixture to milk mixture in pan, stirring with a whisk to combine.

4. Pour mixture into 8 (4-ounce) ovenproof pots de crème cups. Place cups in a 13 x 9-inch baking pan; add hot water to pan to a depth of 1 inch. Bake at 350° for 28 minutes or until a knife inserted in center comes out clean. Remove cups from pan;

cool completely on a wire rack. Chill 8 hours or overnight. Garnish with shaved chocolate, if desired. Yield: 8 servings (serving size: 1 custard).

CALORIES 196 (36% from fat); FAT 7.8g (sat 3.7g, mono 2.7g, poly 0.4g); PROTEIN 5.7g; CARB 31.3g; FIBER 1.9g; CHOL 54mg; IRON 1.0mg; SODIUM 87mg; CALC 106mg

summer

The juice of the grape is the liquid
quintessence of concentrated sunbeams.
—Thomas Love Peacock, English poet and novelist

You can always tell the foods of summer. Their dazzling colors alone are a giveaway to the vivid freshness of their flavors. Bright yellow corn, rich red tomatoes, sunset-colored peaches. Who can resist such expressiveness, such pick-up-with-your-fingers-and-eat appeal? I have to admit I've always thought of summertime cooking as a little oxymoronic, for it seems to me that the best summertime dishes should require little in the way of complex cooking. What makes summer's foods so inviting is their easiness, simplicity, and ability to be sensational when so little is done to them.

Some of summer's best wines have that same quality—a kind of delicious effortlessness. For white wines, that means thirst-quenching quaffers that can just be splashed into a glass, no thought required. The world is full of such white wines, and the

> What makes summer foods so inviting are their easiness, simplicity, and ability to be sensational when so little is done to them.

vast array of fresh summertime foods is the perfect excuse to try a score of them. Unless, of course, a thick steak or some juicy lamb chops are on the grill—and that's when, for me, nothing but a rich red wine will do. In the end, a true "summer kitchen," full of vibrant foods and delicious wines, evokes a feeling of generosity that's impossible to resist.

savoring summer

Served course by course, this delicious menu would be easy to pair with various wines. However, it's somehow more summery to simply put all of these dishes and several wines on the table as one big spread.

menu | wine

menu

White Bean and Bacon Dip with Rosemary Pita Chips

Tomato, Basil, and Fresh Mozzarella Salad

Grilled Chicken with White Barbecue Sauce

Succotash Salad

Two-Potato Salad with Crème Fraîche

Vanilla-Buttermilk Ice Cream

Serves 8

wine

With this menu, the challenge is to find a solitary wine that works well with such a multitude of flavors and textures. But why even try? In keeping with the menu's generous, casual feel, I think it's a lot more exciting (and conversation sparking) to put out two or three different wines.

When I'm working with two wines, I choose two whites: a California pinot gris and an Australian chardonnay. The pinot gris has enough body to stand up to every dish here. At the same time, its refreshing citrusy acidity is a crisp contrast to the barbecue sauce and creamy potato salad. The chardonnay is rounder and fuller in body than the pinot gris. Its butteriness is fabulous with corn, bacon, and beans (white and lima). So for this menu two wines make sense, and guests usually end up liking each for different reasons. Two top picks that have summer-casual price tags are **J Vineyards & Winery Pinot Gris** ($$), from California's Russian River Valley, and **Wolf Blass "President's Selection" Chardonnay** ($$), from South Australia.

If three wines are in order, I add a red zinfandel. Jammy, lip-smacking, and packed with boysenberry, blackberry, and blueberry flavors, zinfandel is an immediate-gratification kind of red. In summer, it's a magical match for barbecued chicken. One of my favorites is **Jeff Runquist Wines "Massoni Ranch" Zinfandel** ($$), from Amador County, California.

Finally, you must have this tangy Vanilla-Buttermilk Ice Cream with a glass of Amontillado Sherry, from Spain. Full of the joys of hazelnut, caramel, and brown sugar, the amontillado is the flavor equivalent of sundae toppings and is, therefore, exquisite with ice cream. Try **Domecq Medium Dry Amontillado Sherry** ($), from Jerez, Spain.

J Vineyards & Winery Pinot Gris

Wolf Blass "President's Selection" Chardonnay

Jeff Runquist Wines "Massoni Ranch" Zinfandel

Domecq Medium Dry Amontillado Sherry

White Bean and Bacon Dip
with Rosemary Pita Chips

Tomato, Basil, and Fresh Mozzarella Salad

In this classic salad, infused vegetable broth provides the base for a basil sauce that stands in for traditional vinaigrette. For the best flavor, use tomatoes from the farmers' market or heirloom tomatoes.

J Vineyards & Winery Pinot Gris

BASIL SAUCE:

    1   cup loosely packed fresh basil leaves
    ⅓   cup vegetable broth
    ¼   cup balsamic vinegar
    1   teaspoon sea salt

SALAD:

    12 (¼-inch-thick) slices ripe yellow
        tomato (1½ pounds)
    12 (¼-inch-thick) slices ripe red tomato
        (1½ pounds)
    ½   cup (2 ounces) shredded fresh
        room-temperature mozzarella cheese
    1   teaspoon freshly ground black pepper
    ½   cup thinly sliced fresh basil

1. To prepare basil sauce, cook 1 cup basil leaves in boiling water 15 seconds; drain. Plunge basil into ice water; drain and pat dry. Combine basil and broth in a blender; process until smooth. Let mixture stand 2 hours at room temperature. Strain through a fine sieve into a bowl; discard solids. Add vinegar and salt, stirring with a whisk.

2. To prepare salad, arrange yellow and red tomato slices alternately on a large platter. Drizzle with basil sauce; sprinkle with cheese and pepper. Top with sliced basil. Serve immediately. Yield: 8 servings (serving size: 3 slices tomato, about 1 tablespoon basil sauce, and 1 tablespoon cheese).

CALORIES 60 (32% from fat); FAT 2.1g (sat 1.1g, mono 0.6g, poly 0.3g); PROTEIN 3.2g; CARB 8.4g; FIBER 2.0g; CHOL 6mg; IRON 1.2mg; SODIUM 369mg; CALC 70mg

White Bean and Bacon Dip with Rosemary Pita Chips

The homemade rosemary-flecked chips are a great complement to the garlicky dip.

Wolf Blass "President's Selection" Chardonnay

CHIPS:

    ½   teaspoon dried crushed rosemary
    ¼   teaspoon salt
    ¼   teaspoon garlic powder
    ⅛   teaspoon freshly ground black pepper
    3   (6-inch) pitas, each cut into 8 wedges
    Cooking spray

DIP:

    2   slices smoked bacon, chopped
    4   garlic cloves, minced
    ⅓   cup fat-free, less-sodium chicken broth
    1   (19-ounce) can cannellini beans or
        other white beans, drained
    ¼   cup chopped green onions
    1   tablespoon fresh lemon juice
    ½   teaspoon hot sauce
    ⅛   teaspoon salt
    ⅛   teaspoon paprika

1. Preheat oven to 350°.

2. To prepare chips, combine first 4 ingredients in a small bowl. Arrange pita wedges in a single layer on a baking sheet. Lightly coat pita wedges with cooking spray; sprinkle evenly with rosemary mixture. Lightly recoat pita wedges with cooking spray. Bake at 350° for 20 minutes or until golden.

3. To prepare dip, cook bacon in a medium saucepan over medium heat until crisp. Remove bacon from pan with a slotted spoon; crumble. Add garlic to drippings in pan; sauté 1 minute. Add broth and beans; bring to a boil. Reduce heat, and simmer, uncovered, 10 minutes.

4. Combine bean mixture, onions, and remaining 4 ingredients in a food processor, and process until smooth. Spoon mixture into a bowl; stir in 1 tablespoon reserved bacon. Sprinkle dip with remaining bacon just before serving. Serve with pita chips. Yield: 8 servings (serving size: 3 pita chips and 3 tablespoons dip).

CALORIES 137 (25% from fat); FAT 3.8g (sat 1.3g, mono 1.5g, poly 0.7g); PROTEIN 4.7g; CARB 20.5g; FIBER 2.6g; CHOL 4mg; IRON 1.4mg; SODIUM 397mg; CALC 39mg

Tomato, Basil, and Fresh
Mozzarella Salad

Succotash Salad, Grilled Chicken with
White Barbecue Sauce

Grilled Chicken with White Barbecue Sauce

Instead of a sweet tomato-based sauce, this grilled chicken is served with a tangy white barbecue sauce.

J Vineyards & Winery Pinot Gris or Jeff Runquist Wines "Massoni Ranch" Zinfandel

CHICKEN:

- 8 (8-ounce) bone-in chicken breast halves
- 1 teaspoon salt
- 1 teaspoon onion powder
- 1 teaspoon garlic powder
- 1 teaspoon paprika
- 1 teaspoon chipotle chile powder
- Cooking spray

SAUCE:

- ½ cup light mayonnaise
- ⅓ cup white balsamic vinegar
- 1 tablespoon coarsely ground black pepper
- 1½ teaspoons fresh lemon juice
- ½ teaspoon ground red pepper
- Dash of salt

1. Prepare grill to medium-hot using both burners.

2. To prepare chicken, loosen skin from breasts by inserting fingers, gently pushing between skin and meat. Combine salt and next 4 ingredients; rub under loosened skin.

3. Coat grill rack with cooking spray. Turn left burner off (leave right burner on). Place chicken on grill rack over right burner; grill 5 to 7 minutes on each side or until browned. Move chicken to grill rack over left burner. Cover and cook 35 minutes or until done, turning once.

4. To prepare sauce, combine mayonnaise and remaining 5 ingredients, stirring with a whisk. Serve with chicken. Remove skin from chicken, if desired (skin not included

in nutrient analysis). Yield: 8 servings (serving size: 1 breast half and about 2 tablespoons sauce).

CALORIES 252 (25% from fat); FAT 6.9g (sat 1.3g, mono 1.4g, poly 3.4g); PROTEIN 34.4g; CARB 10.9g; FIBER 0.6g; CHOL 91mg; IRON 1.5mg; SODIUM 536mg; CALC 26mg

Succotash Salad

A favorite in the southern part of the United States, succotash is a cooked dish of lima beans, corn, and sweet peppers. This version is chilled and tossed with a zesty mustard dressing.

Wolf Blass "President's Selection" Chardonnay

SALAD:

- 1 (16-ounce) bag frozen baby lima beans
- 3 cups fresh corn kernels
- 1 cup chopped red bell pepper
- ¾ cup chopped green onions
- ¼ cup finely chopped red onion
- ¼ cup chopped fresh flat-leaf parsley
- 2 tablespoons chopped fresh oregano

DRESSING:

- ⅓ cup fresh lemon juice
- 2 tablespoons Dijon mustard
- 2 tablespoons olive oil
- ¾ teaspoon salt
- ¾ teaspoon freshly ground black pepper

1. To prepare salad, cook beans in boiling water 12 minutes. Drain; rinse with cold water. Drain. Combine beans, corn, and next 5 ingredients in a bowl.

2. To prepare dressing, combine lemon juice and remaining 4 ingredients, stirring with a whisk. Drizzle over salad, and toss to coat. Yield: 8 servings (serving size: 1 cup).

CALORIES 170 (24% from fat); FAT 4.5g (sat 0.7g, mono 2.9g, poly 0.8g); PROTEIN 6.4g; CARB 29.5g; FIBER 6g; CHOL 0mg; IRON 1.9mg; SODIUM 300mg; CALC 36mg

wine tip

What's the best way to serve several wines during a casual get-together? One could, of course, set the table with multiple wine glasses for each person. To me, however, the "dinner party" approach is too formal for a summery meal such as this. Instead, I put out the wines, give everyone a single glass, and then set out a dump bucket. Despite its somewhat tacky name, a dump bucket is a great piece of wine equipment that allows guests to pour out their last sips of wine, freeing up the glasses for the *next* wine. Almost any large vase, urn, carafe, or pitcher can be used as a dump bucket. Aesthetically, it's best to use something that can't be seen through. A ceramic dump bucket is traditional in Europe, but silver or opaque glass is fine, too. For summery outdoor parties, I like to use a decorative ceramic garden vase or planter set right on the table.

wine tip

You're wondering which dishes are best for serving ice cream. All of a sudden, inspiration strikes: You think that ice cream would look sensational in wine glasses. Bad idea! Virtually all wine glasses are microscopically pitted. Though you can't see the tiny holes on the inside surfaces of the glasses, these indentations trap flavors and aromas left over from other substances, especially from dairy products. Therefore, wine glasses used for serving ice cream have a slight carryover aroma that interferes with the aromas of wine. So no matter how humble your wine glasses, reserve them exclusively for wine.

Two-Potato Salad with Crème Fraîche

Crème fraîche contributes extra creaminess to this potato medley. Look for it near the gourmet cheeses in the supermarket; if you can't find it, substitute full-fat sour cream. You can prepare this dish a day ahead. Stir gently before serving.

J Vineyards & Winery Pinot Gris

1½ pounds small red potatoes, halved
1½ pounds peeled sweet potatoes, cut into
       1-inch pieces
  3 tablespoons white balsamic vinegar
 ¾ cup crème fraîche
 ¼ cup chopped fresh chives
 ¾ teaspoon kosher salt
 ¼ teaspoon freshly ground black
       pepper

1. Place potatoes in a large Dutch oven; cover with water. Bring to a boil; reduce heat, and simmer 18 minutes or until tender. Drain. Place potatoes in a large bowl. Drizzle with vinegar; toss gently to coat. Cool to room temperature.
2. Combine crème fraîche and next 3 ingredients, stirring with a whisk. Add to potatoes, tossing gently to coat. Yield: 8 servings (serving size: 1 cup).

CALORIES 253 (29% from fat); FAT 8.2g (sat 5.0g, mono 2.3g, poly 0.4g); PROTEIN 3.9g; CARB 41.3g; FIBER 3.0g; CHOL 18mg; IRON 1.2mg; SODIUM 255mg; CALC 70mg

Vanilla-Buttermilk Ice Cream

The vanilla bean provides rich flavor for this three-milk ice cream, which is best when served as soon as it's firm.

Domecq Medium Dry Amontillado Sherry

  1 (6-inch) vanilla bean, split lengthwise
  2 cups 2% reduced-fat milk
 ¾ cup sugar
  1 cup low-fat or nonfat buttermilk
  1 (12-ounce) can evaporated fat-free milk

1. Scrap seeds from vanilla bean; place seeds and bean in a heavy saucepan. Pour 2% reduced-fat milk into pan; heat over medium-high heat to 180° or until tiny bubbles form around edge, stirring frequently (do not boil). Remove from heat; discard vanilla bean.
2. Combine vanilla-milk mixture and sugar in a large bowl, stirring until sugar dissolves. Add buttermilk and evaporated milk, stirring until blended; cover and chill completely.
3. Pour mixture into the freezer can of an ice-cream freezer; freeze according to manufacturer's instructions. Spoon ice cream into a freezer-safe container; cover and freeze 1 hour or until firm. Yield: 16 servings (serving size: ½ cup).

CALORIES 76 (11% from fat); FAT 0.9g (sat 0.6g, mono 0.2g, poly 0g); PROTEIN 3.2g; CARB 14.0g; FIBER 0g; CHOL 3mg; IRON 0.1mg; SODIUM 48mg; CALC 118mg

Wine is to the parched mind of man what water is to the sun-drenched plain. It releases the brakes of his self-consciousness and softens the hard-baked crust of dust so that the seeds below may send forth sweet flowers.

—André Simon, French wine authority

Vanilla-Buttermilk Ice Cream

patio dinner

Along the Mediterranean Riviera—in such famous towns as Nice, Cannes, and St. Tropez—the quintessential summer dish is salad niçoise. Just about every café serves it, but only during summer, when vegetables are at their peak of freshness and a glass of cold wine alongside is simply irresistible.

menu | wine

Grilled Salad Niçoise

French bread

Fresh ripe nectarines

Serves 4

Salad niçoise is not so much a salad as it is a protein-rich entrée. Because it's the main attraction, salad niçoise is naturally and inevitably (at least in France) accompanied with wine—usually a wine that embodies the same summery mood as the dish itself. Over the years, I've tried salad niçoise with many different wines, depending on the dish's exact ingredients. Traditionally, of course, the salad combines the season's first tomatoes, waxy potatoes, and green beans in addition to fresh lettuces, lots of garlic, small black briny niçoise olives, and, sometimes, artichokes and eggs. But along the Mediterranean, it's also likely to have first-rate anchovies, either packed in salt or freshly grilled. Grilled tuna, as used in our version, was probably added in the 20th century; today, it has become another classic ingredient.

We've omitted the anchovies (are you glad?) mostly because prime-quality anchovies are hard to find in the United States. Leaving them out has one obvious benefit: The salad goes with more kinds of wine without them. My favorite match—cava, a Spanish sparkling wine made by the Champagne method—may come as a surprise, but it's a superb partner for a multi-ingredient salad. The fresh, lively, clean citrusy exuberance of a cold glass of cava has the effect of "lifting" the salad and making it even livelier. The ultimate carefree bubbly, cava is not expensive. Try the snappy **Segura Viudas "Aria" Brut Cava** ($).

Nectarines are a refreshing finale because, of all the stone fruits, nectarines have the most acidity. I always serve a late harvest sweet riesling with them. Among the crispest of all dessert wines, late harvest rieslings possess a riot of stone-fruit flavors. **Navarro Vineyards Late Harvest White Riesling** ($$ for a 375-milliliter half bottle), from the Anderson Valley of California, is nothing short of voluptuous.

Segura Viudas "Aria" Brut Cava

Navarro Vineyards Late Harvest White Riesling

Grilled Salad Niçoise

Fresh tuna and niçoise olives are the stars of this classic salad. Fresh herbs and vegetables are also essential.

Segura Viudas "Aria" Brut Cava

> 4 cups cubed red potato (about 1¼ pounds)
> ½ pound green beans, trimmed
> 1 (8-ounce) ahi tuna steak (about ¾ inch thick)
> Cooking spray
> ½ cup chopped fresh parsley
> ¼ cup vertically sliced red onion
> 1 tablespoon chopped fresh tarragon
> ½ cup fat-free, less-sodium chicken broth
> 2 tablespoons balsamic vinegar
> 1 tablespoon extravirgin olive oil
> 1 tablespoon Dijon mustard
> ¼ teaspoon salt
> ¼ teaspoon freshly ground black pepper
> 8 cups gourmet salad greens
> 1 cup cherry tomatoes, halved
> ¼ cup niçoise olives

1. Cook potato in boiling water 6 minutes or until tender; remove with a slotted spoon. Add green beans to boiling water, and cook 3 minutes or until crisp-tender. Drain.

2. Prepare grill or broiler.

3. Place fish on a grill rack or broiler pan coated with cooking spray; cook 3 minutes on each side or until desired degree of doneness. Remove skin, and cut fish into 1-inch chunks.

4. Combine potato, fish, parsley, onion, and tarragon in a large bowl. Combine broth and next 5 ingredients; stir well with a whisk. Pour ½ cup broth mixture over potato mixture, and toss well.

5. Divide beans, greens, and tomatoes evenly among 4 plates. Top each serving with 1½ cups potato mixture and 1 tablespoon olives. Drizzle 1 tablespoon of remaining broth mixture over each serving. Yield: 4 servings.

CALORIES 299 (26% from fat); FAT 8.6g (sat 1.6g, mono 4.8g, poly 1.8g); PROTEIN 19.8g; CARB 37.2g; FIBER 6.9g; CHOL 21mg; IRON 4.7mg; SODIUM 458mg; CALC 104mg

about the wine

Cava is the name the Spanish give to a sparkling wine made by the traditional Champagne method—that is, each bottle of wine gets its bubbles naturally by undergoing a second fermentation in that bottle (as opposed to lower-quality sparklers, which are usually injected with carbon dioxide). What's amazing about cava—besides the fact that it's a steal— is its versatility with food, as well as the spirit in which people drink it. No occasion is needed for this bubbly. Historically, in Spain—and, increasingly, all over the world—people drink cava at the drop of a hat.

Jamaican Jerk Turkey Burgers
with Papaya-Mango Salsa

burger cookout

If anything can be dressed up in a new and delicious way, it's the good ol' all-American burger. Here, a summery salsa does the trick by giving the burger a tropical, exotic slant that's refreshing and fun. When you serve the Blackberry-Lemon Upside-Down Cake, be prepared to have no leftovers.

menu | wine

Jamaican Jerk Turkey Burgers with Papaya-Mango Salsa

Grilled Vegetable Salad with Tropical Vinaigrette

Baked tortilla chips

Blackberry-Lemon Upside-Down Cake

Serves 4

Serving a good wine, instead of beer, with burgers is a little like wearing shoes instead of sneakers with jeans. It's still relaxed, still friendly, just a bit ... better. And, I submit, a whole lot more delicious. Plus, this burger is not your standard beef-with-ketchup proposition. First, it's made with ground turkey, which is more mildly flavored and more wine-flexible than beef. Second, the seasonings in this dish are kaleidoscopic: There's sweet and sour from the sauce, spice from the jerk seasoning, citrus from the lime, a tropical sense from the mango and papaya, and a touch of herb from the cilantro. Each of these seasonings balances the others in perfect point-counterpoint fashion. The question is, which wine will then counterbalance all of them?

The answer? Gewürztraminer, a bold, extroverted white wine that's raging with fruitiness and every bit up to the challenge of pairing with monolithic flavors. Because it's summer, I've chosen one of my favorite lightish bodied gewürztraminers: **Chateau Ste. Michelle Gewürztraminer** ($), from the Columbia Valley of Washington State. Lip-smacking, exotic, vibrant, and fresh, this gewürztraminer is also a terrific partner for the citrusy, tropical-dressed grilled vegetable salad.

With its soft pound cake-like texture, burst of berryness, and hint of lemony zing, Blackberry-Lemon Upside-Down Cake is a simple yet striking end to this summer meal. I serve it with small glasses of very cold **Bonny Doon Vineyard Muscat Vin de Glacière** ($$ for a 375-milliliter half bottle), one of the most exuberant dessert wines made in California. The wine's outrageously vibrant berry, apricot, citrus, and pineapple flavors will send shivers up and down your spine.

Chateau Ste. Michelle Gewürztraminer

Bonny Doon Vineyard Muscat Vin de Glacière

Jamaican Jerk Turkey Burgers with Papaya-Mango Salsa

Burgers on the grill are anything but ordinary when they're made with jerk-seasoned ground turkey. The cool, fruity salsa offsets the spice of the burgers.

Chateau Ste. Michelle Gewürztraminer

SALSA:
- ⅔ cup diced peeled papaya
- ⅔ cup diced peeled mango
- ¼ cup finely chopped red bell pepper
- 2 tablespoons chopped fresh cilantro
- ½ teaspoon grated lime rind
- 2 tablespoons fresh lime juice
- 1 tablespoon minced sweet onion

BURGERS:
- ½ cup minced sweet onion
- ½ cup dry breadcrumbs
- ⅓ cup bottled sweet-and-sour simmer sauce (such as Kikkoman)
- ¼ cup finely chopped red bell pepper
- 1 tablespoon Jamaican jerk seasoning
- 1 large egg white
- 1 pound ground turkey
- Cooking spray
- 4 (2-ounce) Kaiser rolls

1. To prepare salsa, combine first 7 ingredients. Let stand at room temperature at least 30 minutes.

2. Prepare grill to medium heat.

3. To prepare burgers, combine ½ cup onion and next 5 ingredients, stirring well. Add turkey; mix well to combine. Divide turkey mixture into 4 equal portions, shaping each into a 1-inch-thick patty. Cover and refrigerate 20 minutes.

4. Lightly coat patties with cooking spray; place on a grill rack coated with cooking spray. Grill 7 minutes on each side or until done.

5. Cut rolls in half horizontally. Place rolls, cut sides down, on grill rack; grill 1 minute or until lightly toasted. Place 1 patty on bottom half of each roll; top with ½ cup salsa and top half of roll. Yield: 4 servings (serving size: 1 burger).

CALORIES 424 (22% from fat); FAT 10.4g (sat 2.5g, mono 3.7g, poly 2.9g); PROTEIN 24.1g; CARB 58.0g; FIBER 3.9g; CHOL 67mg; IRON 4mg; SODIUM 818mg; CALC 121mg

Grilled Vegetable Salad with Tropical Vinaigrette

Grilling just seems to bring out the best flavor in summer vegetables. This is a smart make-ahead dish because the vegetables can be grilled a few hours prior to assembling the salads.

Chateau Ste. Michelle Gewürztraminer

VINAIGRETTE:
- 3 tablespoons fresh orange juice
- 1½ tablespoons papaya juice
- 2½ teaspoons extravirgin olive oil
- 2 teaspoons honey
- 1 teaspoon balsamic vinegar
- ¼ teaspoon salt
- ⅛ teaspoon freshly ground black pepper

SALAD:
- ¼ pound carrots, peeled and cut diagonally into ½-inch-thick pieces
- ¼ pound green beans, trimmed
- ¼ pound sugar snap peas, trimmed
- ¼ cup (½-inch-thick) slices red onion
- Cooking spray
- ½ teaspoon freshly ground black pepper
- ¼ teaspoon kosher salt
- 6 cups torn romaine lettuce
- ½ cup thinly sliced radishes (optional)

1. To prepare vinaigrette, combine first 7 ingredients, stirring with a whisk until well blended. Cover and chill.

2. Prepare grill to medium heat.

3. To prepare salad, cook carrots in boiling water 2 minutes, add beans and peas, and cook 3 minutes or until crisp-tender. Drain and plunge into ice water; drain. Place mixture in a large bowl, and add onion slices. Lightly coat vegetable mixture with cooking spray. Sprinkle with ½ teaspoon pepper and salt; gently toss to coat.

4. Place vegetable mixture in a wire grilling basket coated with cooking spray. Place grilling basket on grill rack, and grill 7 minutes on each side or until lightly browned. Arrange lettuce on salad plates. Divide grilled vegetables and, if desired, radishes evenly among servings. Drizzle each salad with vinaigrette. Yield: 4 servings (serving size: 1½ cups lettuce, ¼ of vegetables, and 1 tablespoon vinaigrette).

CALORIES 101 (29% from fat); FAT 3.3g (sat 0.5g, mono 2.3g, poly 0.4g); PROTEIN 2.5g; CARB 15.3g; FIBER 4.5g; CHOL 0mg; IRON 1.4mg; SODIUM 293mg; CALC 69mg

good cook tip

There are several great strategies for making any salad more wine-friendly: First, grill vegetables rather than serving them raw. Grilling caramelizes a vegetable's natural sugars, causing the vegetable to taste mellower, richer, and less vegetal, thereby upping its affinity with wine. Second, always use a "soft" vinegar. Wine vinegar, for example, is not ideal because it's so harsh that it makes the wine taste strident and bitter. By comparison, balsamic and Sherry vinegars are mellower and far more wine-friendly. Another great idea is to reduce the amount of vinegar used by adding some fruit juice (orange, passion fruit, papaya, or peach) as an acidifying agent.

Grilled Vegetable Salad with
Tropical Vinaigrette

Blackberry-Lemon Upside-Down Cake

Juicy summer blackberries elevate this upside-down cake from simple to sublime.

Bonny Doon Vineyard Muscat Vin de Glacière

  2 teaspoons butter
  1/3 cup packed brown sugar
  1 cup fresh blackberries
  1 1/2 teaspoons grated lemon rind
  1 1/4 cups all-purpose flour
  1 1/2 teaspoons baking powder
  1/4 teaspoon salt
  2/3 cup granulated sugar
  2 tablespoons butter, softened
  1 large egg
  3/4 teaspoon vanilla extract
  1/2 cup fat-free milk

1. Preheat oven to 350°.

2. Melt 2 teaspoons butter in a 9-inch round cake pan. Sprinkle brown sugar over melted butter; return to oven, and bake 1 to 2 minutes or until sugar melts. Top with blackberries and lemon rind; set aside.

3. Lightly spoon flour into dry measuring cups; level with a knife. Combine flour, baking powder, and salt in a small bowl.

4. Place granulated sugar and 2 tablespoons butter in a large bowl; beat with a mixer at medium speed until well blended. Add egg and vanilla; beat well. Add flour mixture to egg mixture alternately with milk, beginning and ending with flour mixture; mix after each addition. Spoon batter over blackberries.

5. Bake at 350° for 35 to 40 minutes or until a wooden pick inserted in center comes out clean. Cool in pan 5 minutes on a wire rack. Loosen edges of cake with a knife. Place a plate upside down on top of cake pan; invert onto plate. Yield: 8 servings (serving size: 1 wedge).

CALORIES 229 (18% from fat); FAT 4.7g (sat 2.2g, mono 1.8g, poly 0.4g); PROTEIN 3.7g; CARB 43.4g; FIBER 0.6g; CHOL 37mg; IRON 1.4mg; SODIUM 214mg; CALC 94mg

about the wine

Bonny Doon Vineyard Muscat Vin de Glacière is made in one of the zaniest manners of any dessert wine: The grapes are picked ripe, as normal grapes would be, and then they are chilled to 10°F in a huge industrial freezer. (It's a way, in sunny California, of approximating ice wine.) Once frozen rock hard, the grapes are gently pressed until just the concentrated juice trickles out, leaving the water in the grapes behind in the form of ice.

waterside dinner

The fresh green flavors of these savory dishes remind me of summer days by the sea, watching boats rock on the waves and smelling—almost *tasting*—the salty, briny air. The right wine for this food (and for this mood) is cold, fresh, and a touch green, too—at least until dessert.

menu | wine

menu

Roasted Fig and Arugula Salad

Grilled Lemon-Bay Shrimp

Barley Risotto with Fennel and Olives

Herbed Cracker Bread

—

Cherries in Zinfandel Syrup

Serves 4

wine

Figs, arugula, lemon, bay, fennel, and olives—key ingredients in these dishes—also happen to be common descriptors of the myriad green flavors in sauvignon blanc. So sauvignon blanc is the perfect choice to serve here. It's not just that the wine mirrors the food and vice versa. When flavors line up as synergistically as this, it's almost as if the actual molecules of flavor reverberate, creating a hypnotic sensation that is all-consuming—the taste equivalent of being surrounded by stereophonic music.

Which sauvignon blanc to serve is the question, for delicious sauvignon blancs are made all over the globe. My answer is to use this opportunity to have a mini wine tasting during dinner. I serve three different sauvignon blancs from three distinctly different places—such as France, South Africa, and New Zealand—to make the tasting more dramatic and fun. **Pascal Jolivet Sancerre** ($$), from France, (Sancerre is 100 percent sauvignon blanc) is tangy, supercrisp, and light. South African sauvignons—such as **Neil Ellis** ($$), from Groenekloof—are smokier and more green tea-like and intense. And a good New Zealand sauvignon blanc, such as **Lawson's Dry Hills** ($), is off the charts with outrageously green flavors. To make it a more extensive tasting, add an excellent Chilean sauvignon blanc, such as **Veramonte** ($), and one from California, such as **Kunde** ($).

The idea of closely tying flavors together moves up a notch when the cherries arrive. Here, the wine I use in the dessert is the same as the wine I serve with it: **Rosenblum Cellars "Rosie Rabbit Vineyard" Late Harvest Zinfandel** ($$ for a 375-milliliter half bottle). This is a powerfully intense cherry dessert that underscores (and is underscored by) the intensity of the late harvest zinfandel itself.

Pascal Jolivet Sancerre

Neil Ellis Sauvignon Blanc

Lawson's Dry Hills Sauvignon Blanc

Rosenblum Cellars "Rosie Rabbit Vineyard" Late Harvest Zinfandel

Grilled Lemon-Bay Shrimp

Fresh bay leaves and lemon wedges infuse peppered shrimp with woodsy and citrusy flavors in this simple dish.

Pascal Jolivet Sancerre, Neil Ellis Sauvignon Blanc, and Lawson's Dry Hills Sauvignon Blanc

  2 tablespoons fresh lemon juice
  1 tablespoon olive oil
  ½ teaspoon salt
  ½ teaspoon crushed red pepper
  ½ teaspoon freshly ground black pepper
  2 garlic cloves, minced
 32 large shrimp, peeled and deveined
 16 to 32 fresh bay leaves
  4 large lemons, each cut into 8 wedges
Cooking spray

1. Prepare grill.
2. Combine first 6 ingredients in a large bowl. Add shrimp; toss to coat. Cover and marinate in refrigerator 10 minutes.
3. Place bay leaves and lemon wedges in a bowl. Coat with cooking spray; toss. Thread 4 lemon wedges, 4 shrimp, and 2 to 4 bay leaves alternately onto each of 8 skewers. Place on grill rack coated with cooking spray; grill 2 minutes on each side or until shrimp are done. Discard bay leaves. Yield: 4 servings (serving size: 2 skewers).

CALORIES 217 (27% from fat); FAT 6.4g (sat 1.0g, mono 2.9g, poly 1.4g); PROTEIN 34.8g; CARB 3.1g; FIBER 0.3g; CHOL 259mg; IRON 4.3mg; SODIUM 545mg; CALC 94mg

Roasted Fig and Arugula Salad

Roasting slightly caramelizes the figs and creates flavorful browned bits that eventually season the vinaigrette. If you don't have molasses on hand, use honey.

Pascal Jolivet Sancerre, Neil Ellis Sauvignon Blanc, and Lawson's Dry Hills Sauvignon Blanc

  ⅓ cup Sherry vinegar or cider vinegar
  1 tablespoon molasses
  2 teaspoons extravirgin olive oil
  ¼ teaspoon salt
  4 large (dark-skinned) fresh figs, halved
Cooking spray
  5 cups trimmed arugula
  ¼ cup (1 ounce) crumbled goat cheese
  ⅛ teaspoon freshly ground black pepper

1. Preheat oven to 425°.
2. Combine first 4 ingredients in a medium bowl, stirring with a whisk. Add figs; toss to coat. Remove figs with a slotted spoon, reserving vinegar mixture.
3. Place figs in a cast-iron or ovenproof skillet coated with cooking spray. Bake at 425° for 8 to 10 minutes. Remove figs from pan; place on a plate. Immediately add reserved vinegar mixture to hot pan, scraping pan to loosen browned bits. Pour into a small bowl; cool figs and vinaigrette to room temperature.
4. Place arugula on a platter; arrange figs over arugula. Sprinkle with cheese and pepper. Drizzle with cooled vinaigrette. Yield: 4 servings (serving size: 1¼ cups).

CALORIES 109 (34% from fat); FAT 4.1g (sat 1.4g, mono 2.1g, poly 0.4g); PROTEIN 2.4g; CARB 18.0g; FIBER 2.5g; CHOL 3mg; IRON 1.1mg; SODIUM 182mg; CALC 84mg

about the wine

Sauvignon blanc works with virtually any dish that has green flavors because the wine itself has a greenness that's expressed in a multitude of ways. A good sauvignon, for example, can be evocative of limes, freshly cut grass, green tea, spearmint, arugula, green olives, snow peas, lemongrass, green figs, honeydew melon, sage, and Key lime pie.

Grilled Lemon-Bay Shrimp

wine tip

What about cooking with wine? When added as an ingredient in a dish, wine has one purpose only: to add extra dimension, complexity, and depth to flavors. In fact, without wine, a risotto like the one here would simply not have the same kind of deliciousness. Given its importance, then, the wine you use must be a good one. A poor-quality wine—or one that's been hanging around the kitchen too long—will only contribute sour, bitter flavors to the dish. Master chef Julia Child once said, "If you do not have a good wine to use, it is far better to omit it, for a poor one can spoil a simple dish and utterly debase a noble one." The simple rule of all good cooks who love wine? If you wouldn't drink it, don't cook with it!

Barley Risotto with Fennel and Olives

Instead of Arborio rice, this risotto features hearty, nutty-tasting barley. Oil-cured olives offer a savory, rich flavor.

Pascal Jolivet Sancerre, Neil Ellis Sauvignon Blanc, and Lawson's Dry Hills Sauvignon Blanc

  1 tablespoon butter
1½ cups chopped leek, divided
  1 cup finely chopped fennel bulb, divided
  ½ cup finely chopped red bell pepper
  ¾ cup uncooked pearl barley
  1 teaspoon fresh or ¼ teaspoon dried thyme
  2 garlic cloves, minced
3½ cups fat-free, less-sodium chicken broth, divided
  ½ cup sauvignon blanc
  ⅓ cup (about 1½ ounces) grated fresh Parmigiano-Reggiano cheese
  ¼ cup chopped fresh parsley
  1 teaspoon freshly ground black pepper
  ¼ cup oil-cured olives, pitted and chopped
    Chopped fennel fronds (optional)

1. Melt butter in a large saucepan over medium-high heat. Add ¾ cup leek, ½ cup fennel, and bell pepper; sauté 5 minutes or until tender. Add barley, thyme, and garlic; cook 2 minutes, stirring constantly. Stir in 2 cups broth, and cook 10 minutes or until liquid is nearly absorbed, stirring constantly. Stir in ¾ cup leek, ½ cup fennel, 1½ cups broth, and wine; cook until liquid is nearly absorbed, stirring frequently (about 45 minutes). Stir in cheese, parsley, and black pepper. Sprinkle with olives; garnish with fennel fronds, if desired. Yield: 4 servings (serving size: ¾ cup).

CALORIES 255 (26% from fat); FAT 7.5g (sat 3.8g, mono 2.4g, poly 0.7g); PROTEIN 12.1g; CARB 36.1g; FIBER 8.2g; CHOL 15mg; IRON 3.1mg; SODIUM 693mg; CALC 192mg

Herbed Cracker Bread

Ideal with Roasted Fig and Arugula Salad (page 78), these irregularly shaped cheesy crackers are brimming with rich herb and pepper flavors. Vary the flavor by using other dried herbs in place of herbes de Provence; I especially like to use rosemary or basil.

Pascal Jolivet Sancerre, Neil Ellis Sauvignon Blanc, and Lawson's Dry Hills Sauvignon Blanc

  2 cups all-purpose flour
  ⅓ cup (about 1½ ounces) grated fresh Parmigiano-Reggiano cheese
  2 teaspoons dried herbes de Provence
1½ teaspoons coarsely ground black pepper
  1 teaspoon baking powder
  1 teaspoon sugar
  ¾ teaspoon salt
  ½ cup fat-free sour cream
  2 tablespoons butter, melted
  1 large egg
    Cooking spray
  3 tablespoons yellow cornmeal

1. Preheat oven to 350°.
2. Lightly spoon flour into dry measuring cups, and level with a knife. Combine flour and next 6 ingredients in a large bowl, stirring with a whisk.
3. Combine sour cream, butter, and egg, stirring with a whisk. Add egg mixture to flour mixture; stir to form a soft dough. Turn dough out onto a lightly floured surface; knead lightly 7 or 8 times.
4. Divide dough in half. Place 1 dough portion on each of 2 baking sheets coated with cooking spray and sprinkled with 1½ tablespoons cornmeal; turn to coat top of dough. Roll each portion into a 12 x 8-inch rectangle (about ⅛ inch thick). Bake at 350° for 15 minutes or until browned and crisp. Remove from pan, and cool completely on wire racks. Break into 24 crackers. Yield: 2 dozen (serving size: 2 crackers).

CALORIES 132 (25% from fat); FAT 3.7g (sat 2.0g, mono 1.0g, poly 0.3g); PROTEIN 4.7g; CARB 19.9g; FIBER 0.9g; CHOL 26mg; IRON 1.4mg; SODIUM 278mg; CALC 89mg

Cherries in Zinfandel Syrup

With notes of berries and pepper from the wine, the spiced syrup and sweet cherries create a perfect balance of flavors.
Rosenblum Cellars "Rosie Rabbit Vineyard" Late Harvest Zinfandel

½   teaspoon grated lemon rind
4   black peppercorns
1   (2-inch) cinnamon stick
1   (3-inch) rosemary sprig
2½ cups late harvest zinfandel
½   cup water
⅓   cup honey
2   tablespoons fresh lemon juice
3   cups pitted sweet cherries
½   (10.75-ounce) loaf pound cake
Cooking spray
⅓   cup reduced-fat sour cream
1   tablespoon honey

1. Place first 4 ingredients on a double layer of cheesecloth. Gather the edges together; tie securely.
2. Combine wine and next 3 ingredients in a saucepan; bring to a boil. Add cheesecloth bag; cook 5 minutes. Reduce heat; add cherries. Simmer 5 minutes, stirring occasionally. Drain cherries, reserving cooking liquid.
3. Place cherries in a bowl; discard cheesecloth. Return cooking liquid to pan; bring to a boil. Cook 20 minutes or until reduced to 1¼ cups. Pour wine syrup over cherries; refrigerate 1½ hours.
4. Preheat oven to 350°. Cut cake into 24 (1-inch) cubes; arrange on a baking sheet coated with cooking spray. Bake at 350° for 12 minutes, turning every 4 minutes.
5. Combine sour cream and 1 tablespoon honey with a whisk. Spoon mixture into glasses; top with croutons and sour cream mixture. Yield: 6 servings (serving size: ½ cup).

CALORIES 195 (29% from fat); FAT 6.2g (sat 2.2g, mono 2.5g, poly 0.6g); PROTEIN 2.2g; CARB 34.7g; FIBER 0.4g; CHOL 22mg; IRON 1mg; SODIUM 118mg; CALC 49mg

Beef Tenderloin with
Warm Vegetable Salad,
Grilled New Potatoes

the thrill of the grill

The definition of summer? Here it is in three phrases: grilled steak, grilled vegetables, grilled fruit. Grilling, mankind's first cooking technique, is still possibly the most satisfying way to cook—especially when you're sipping a phenomenal wine at the same time.

menu | wine

Beef Tenderloin with Warm Vegetable Salad

Grilled New Potatoes

Garlic-Herb French Bread

Grilled Peaches

Serves 4

In the history of famous wine-and-food marriages, there have always been classic pairings. And here's one that's unabashedly, irrevocably American: grilled steak and cabernet sauvignon. A really good cabernet sauvignon tastes so incredible with a thick juicy slice of grilled beef because the wine has immense structure and what's often called "grip." This powerful, mouthfilling character has textural affinity with the meaty, dense, sink-your-teeth-into-this texture of grilled beef. Also, cabernet sauvignon's deep, cassislike flavors nicely counterbalance the deep, rich flavor of beef. In addition, a great grilled steak's appeal comes in part from its charred crust, a flavor that is thoroughly harmonious with cabernet sauvignon, since top cabernets are aged (usually for at least two years) in toasted (charred) new oak barrels. Finally, cabernet sauvignon often has an underlying hint of rosemary, mint, and/or oregano. When any of these herbs are used—as they are with the tenderloin and potatoes—cabernet sauvignon provides a seamless match.

With these dishes, I like to drink a really top-notch cabernet from California's Napa Valley, renowned for its full-throttle versions. I have many favorites: Shafer, Paradigm, Dalle Valle, and dozens of others. But I often serve one that I know really well: **Fife Vineyards Reserve Cabernet Sauvignon** ($$$$), from Spring Mountain District. It's a small vineyard, but my husband owns it.

As summer desserts go, it's hard to top the purity of a plain ripe peach. But after the satisfaction of grilled steak, the opulent flavor of vanilla-laced Grilled Peaches is, well, perfect. Try them with the lavishly peachy **Dolce** ($$$$$ for a 375-milliliter half bottle), from the Napa Valley, a richly sublime dessert wine that spreads over your taste buds like liquefied honey.

Fife Vineyards Reserve Cabernet Sauvignon

Dolce

Beef Tenderloin with Warm Vegetable Salad

Fresh summer vegetables, grilled and tossed with olive oil and oregano, are a tasty and colorful accompaniment to the steak.

Fife Vineyards Reserve Cabernet Sauvignon

  4 (4-ounce) beef tenderloin steaks, trimmed (about 1 inch thick)
  ½ teaspoon kosher salt, divided
  ½ teaspoon black pepper, divided
  2 tablespoons balsamic vinegar
  2 teaspoons minced garlic
  2 small zucchini, halved lengthwise
  2 small yellow squash, halved lengthwise
  2 plum tomatoes, halved lengthwise
  2 green onions
     Cooking spray
  2 teaspoons olive oil
  2 teaspoons minced oregano

1. Prepare grill or broiler.
2. Sprinkle steaks with ¼ teaspoon salt and ¼ teaspoon pepper.
3. Combine ¼ teaspoon salt, ¼ teaspoon pepper, vinegar, and next 5 ingredients in a large zip-top plastic bag. Seal bag, and shake to coat.
4. Place zucchini and yellow squash on grill rack or broiler pan coated with cooking spray; cook 3 minutes on each side or until tender. Place tomato and onions on grill rack or broiler pan; cook 2 minutes or just until tender.
5. Coarsely chop vegetables, and place in a bowl. Add olive oil and minced oregano; stir gently.
6. Place tenderloin steaks on grill rack or broiler pan coated with cooking spray; cook 4 minutes on each side or until desired degree of doneness. Serve steaks with vegetable mixture. Yield: 4 servings (serving size: 1 steak and ½ cup vegetable mixture).

CALORIES 203 (36% from fat); FAT 8.2g (sat 2.4g, mono 3.9g, poly 0.6g); PROTEIN 24.1g; CARB 7.5g; FIBER 1.8g; CHOL 52mg; IRON 2.1mg; SODIUM 354mg; CALC 43mg

Grilled New Potatoes

Simply seasoned red potatoes take on a whole new dimension of flavor when they're cooked on the grill.

Fife Vineyards Reserve Cabernet Sauvignon

  1½ pounds small red potatoes, halved
  1 teaspoon kosher salt
  2 teaspoons olive oil
     Cooking spray

1. Prepare grill.
2. Toss potatoes with salt and olive oil.
3. Place potatoes ¼ inch apart on a grill rack coated with cooking spray. Grill 15 minutes; turn over with tongs. Grill an additional 15 minutes or until done. Cool slightly. Yield: 4 servings (serving size: 1 cup).

CALORIES 144 (16% from fat); FAT 2.6g (sat 0.4g, mono 1.8g, poly 0.3g); PROTEIN 3.2g; CARB 27.1g; FIBER 2.9g; CHOL 0mg; IRON 1.2mg; SODIUM 481mg; CALC 17mg

Garlic-Herb French Bread

Perk up a basic baguette with some garlic and basil.

Fife Vineyards Reserve Cabernet Sauvignon

  ½ French baguette (about 6 ounces)
     Olive oil-flavored cooking spray
  ½ teaspoon garlic powder
  ½ teaspoon dried basil

1. Prepare grill.
2. Cut a baguette into ½-inch-thick slices. Coat bread with olive oil-flavored cooking spray; sprinkle with garlic powder and basil. Place bread on grill rack coated with cooking spray; grill uncovered, 5 minutes or until crisp. Yield: 4 servings (serving size: 1 slice).

CALORIES 137 (17% from fat); FAT 2.6g (sat 0.3g, mono 0.9g, poly 0.7g); PROTEIN 4.2g; CARB 24.6g; FIBER 1.6g; CHOL 0mg; IRON 1.3mg; SODIUM 281mg; CALC 38mg

Grilled Peaches

Vanilla and black pepper heighten the sweetness of the peaches. Keep in mind that firm fruit holds up best on the grill.

Dolce

  1½ tablespoons white balsamic vinegar
  1 tablespoon extravirgin olive oil
  1 tablespoon fresh lime juice
  ½ tablespoon brown sugar
  1 teaspoon vanilla extract
  ⅛ teaspoon freshly ground black pepper
     Dash of salt
     Dash of hot sauce
  1½ pounds firm peaches, halved and pitted (about 4 peaches)
     Cooking spray

1. Prepare grill.
2. Combine first 8 ingredients in a small bowl, stirring well with a whisk.
3. Place peaches on grill rack coated with cooking spray; grill 3 minutes on each side. Remove from grill. Drizzle peaches with dressing. Yield: 4 servings (serving size: 2 peach halves and 1 tablespoon vinaigrette).

CALORIES 129 (29% from fat); FAT 4.1g (sat 0.5g, mono 2.9g, poly 0.4g); PROTEIN 1.4g; CARB 23.8g; FIBER 2.9g; CHOL 0mg; IRON 0.3mg; SODIUM 39mg; CALC 12mg

about the wine

Many of the world's most sensual dessert wines (including Dolce) are made with the help of *Botrytis cinerea*, the so-called "noble rot" that makes French Sauternes possible. The beneficial *Botrytis* mold spores shrivel the grapes so that the sweet juice inside becomes progressively more concentrated. When the grapes are finally picked and pressed, a wine of incredible lushness results.

Grilled Peaches

italian farmhouse supper

About twenty years ago, I was served a pasta dish (much like the one featured here) by the matriarch of the family whose winery I was visiting in Italy. A true Italian grandmother, she'd decided I must be hungry after so much wine tasting. She put the pasta in front of me and poured a glass of simple white wine—then she smiled and left the room. It was an unforgettable meal.

menu | wine

Penne with Tomatoes, Olives, and Capers

Tossed green salad with balsamic vinaigrette

Breadsticks

———

Cantaloupe wedges

Serves 4

Mention the words *Italian wine,* and most of us picture a bottle of Chianti. But dozens of snappy white wines are made in Italy—wines that are fresh, lively, uncomplicated, and just the ticket on a hot summer evening. The Italian white almost everyone knows is pinot grigio, which is a light, clean, utilitarian quaff. To me, it's the "basic white shirt" of wines—good to have around but more serviceable than spectacular. So with a lusty flavor-packed pasta dish, such as this penne, I'd rather have one of Italy's other dry, refreshing whites: vernaccia. Italian legend has it that vernaccia is a wine that "kisses, licks, bites, and stings"—not to mention quenches your thirst! Light bodied with a dry, citrusy, almondy bite, vernaccia stands up perfectly when basil and garlic are in the picture. It also has enough acidity to offset the acidity in the tomatoes as well as the brininess of both the capers and the kalamata olives.

Among the scores of producers, ironically the one I think you should try isn't labeled vernaccia at all: **Teruzzi & Puthod "Terre di Tufi"** ($$) includes other grapes besides vernaccia (chardonnay and vermentino) so the wine is given the proprietary name Terre di Tufi.

An utterly simple Italian dessert, ripe cantaloupe is delicious with the famous northern Italian wine moscato d'Asti. Moscato is delicate, lightly sweet, gorgeously fruity, and low in alcohol (no more than 5.5% by law). It also has the barest hint of effervescence (*frizzante* in Italian), which makes it a lively, fresh partner for the fruit. Italians splash a little of the wine over the cantaloupe, as well as enjoy a glass alongside. One of the best moscatos is **Michele Chiarlo "Nivole" Moscato d'Asti** ($ for a 375-milliliter half bottle).

Teruzzi & Puthod "Terre di Tufi"

Michele Chiarlo "Nivole" Moscato d'Asti

Penne with Tomatoes, Olives, and Capers

This simple dish depends on fresh basil, garlic, and tomatoes to deliver big flavor.

Teruzzi & Puthod "Terre di Tufi"

3 cups uncooked tube-shaped pasta
3 tablespoons extravirgin olive oil
¼ teaspoon crushed red pepper
3 garlic cloves, finely chopped
3 cups chopped plum tomato (about 1¾ pounds)
½ cup chopped pitted kalamata olives
1 tablespoon capers, drained
½ teaspoon salt
¾ cup (3 ounces) grated fresh Parmigiano-Reggiano cheese
½ cup chopped fresh basil

1. Cook pasta according to package directions, omitting salt and fat. Drain.

2. Heat oil in a large nonstick skillet over medium-high heat. Add pepper and garlic; sauté 30 seconds. Add tomato, olives, capers, and salt. Reduce heat, and simmer 8 minutes, stirring occasionally.

3. Add pasta to pan, tossing gently to coat; cook 1 minute or until thoroughly heated. Remove from heat. Sprinkle with cheese and basil. Yield: 4 servings (serving size: about 1¾ cups).

CALORIES 540 (33% from fat); FAT 19.7g (sat 5.8g, mono 11.4g, poly 1.5g); PROTEIN 21.7g; CARB 73.4g; FIBER 5.8g; CHOL 15mg; IRON 4.2mg; SODIUM 880mg; CALC 329mg

wine tip

What would Italian food be without tomatoes—so juicy, so ... acidic. Even ripe tomatoes have a good deal of natural acidity, which gives them their tangy deliciousness. But it also means you have to be careful about which wines you pair with them. Tomatoes actually taste best with wines that mirror their high-acid profile. Acidity gives wine freshness, brightness, and vivacity—just the ticket for tangy tomato dishes. In Italy, tomato-laced pastas are often served with a bracingly crisp dry white, such as vernaccia, pinot grigio, tocai friulano, Gavi, arneis, or vermentino.

Sautéed Button and Porcini Mushrooms,
Rosemary-Grilled Lamb Chops

mediterranean grill

This menu takes much of its inspiration from Spain, where I enjoyed several summers as a young adult. After a day spent visiting *bodegas* (wineries), friends and I would share platters of shrimp and herb-sprinkled lamb chops right off a charcoal grill. All these years later, there's no summer meal I love more.

menu | wine

Shrimp and Fennel in Hot Garlic Sauce

Rosemary-Grilled Lamb Chops

Sautéed Button and Porcini Mushrooms

Peach-Ginger Crisp

Serves 4

In summer, along the bright, white coast of southern Spain, no one would think of having a platter of shrimp with anything besides a chilled glass of manzanilla Sherry. Hauntingly dry and complex, manzanilla Sherry has a dramatic flavor that is often described as sea spray-like. That minerality and freshness is extraordinary when enjoyed between bites of garlicky shrimp and crunchy fennel. My favorite manzanilla is **Hidalgo "La Gitana,"** meaning "gypsy," ($$ for a 500-milliliter bottle).

Hidalgo "La Gitana" Manzanilla Sherry

Lamb is the traditional meat of Spain, as well as much of the Mediterranean. As such, its affinity with Mediterranean wines is centuries old. The rich, earthy flavors of lamb are born for the grill. In particular, lamb chops—among the mildest cuts of lamb—are deliciously enhanced by the sweetness and crusty char that comes from quick-cooking over fire. One of the most sensual wine matches for these chops—especially when accompanied with an earthy sauté of mushrooms—is Rioja, the leading red wine of Spain. Supple in texture, Riojas have lush vanilla-scented berry flavors that are irresistible when served with lamb. Virtually all Riojas are made primarily from tempranillo, which is considered the king of Spanish red wine grapes. A fabulous wine to try is **Baron de Ley "Finca Monasterio" Rioja** ($$$).

Baron de Ley "Finca Monasterio" Rioja

And, finally, is there anything sexier and more summerlike than a Peach-Ginger Crisp? To go with it, I switch to France and serve one of the best-kept secrets of French dessert wines: Quarts de Chaume. Made from chenin blanc grapes, Quarts de Chaume has an aroma of quinces, stone fruits, honey, and citrus. It is not sugary sweet, but rather refined and subtle. I find such a wine as **Domaine des Baumard Quarts de Chaume** ($$$$ for a 375-milliliter half bottle) to be an exquisite backdrop for this fruity, exotic crisp.

Domaine des Baumard Quarts de Chaume

Shrimp and Fennel in Hot Garlic Sauce

When friends come over, I like to make this quick, easy appetizer and serve it family-style on a big white platter. Don't forget to squeeze the lime at the end of the recipe; it's the flavorful ribbon that ties the food and wine together.

Hidalgo "La Gitana" Manzanilla Sherry

    1 tablespoon olive oil
 3 ½ cups thinly sliced fennel bulb (about
         ¾ pound)
    ¼ teaspoon salt
    ⅛ teaspoon freshly ground black pepper
    4 garlic cloves, thinly sliced
    1 bay leaf
    ½ teaspoon crushed red pepper
    ¾ pound large shrimp, peeled and
         deveined
    2 tablespoons fresh lime juice
Lime wedges

1. Heat oil in a large nonstick skillet over medium-high heat. Add sliced fennel, salt, freshly ground black pepper, garlic, and bay leaf; cook 5 minutes or until fennel is crisp-tender, stirring occasionally. Add red pepper and shrimp to pan; cook 3 minutes or until shrimp are done, stirring occasionally. Discard bay leaf. Stir in lime juice. Serve with lime wedges. Yield: 4 servings (serving size: about 1 cup).

CALORIES 154 (30% from fat); FAT 5.1g (sat 0.8g, mono 2.7g, poly 0.9g); PROTEIN 18.6g; CARB 8.8g; FIBER 2.8g; CHOL 129mg; IRON 2.8mg; SODIUM 317mg; CALC 93mg

Rosemary-Grilled Lamb Chops

Just the addition of a few ingredients, such as garlic and chopped fresh rosemary, lend a heady fragrant aroma to humble lamb chops. An instant-read thermometer is helpful for determining when to remove the lamb from the grill (from 140° for rare to 170° for well done).
Baron de Ley "Finca Monasterio" Rioja

1   tablespoon chopped fresh rosemary
1   teaspoon olive oil
½   teaspoon kosher salt, divided
1   garlic clove, minced
8   (4-ounce) lamb loin chops, trimmed
⅛   teaspoon freshly ground black pepper
Cooking spray
Rosemary sprigs (optional)

1. Combine rosemary, oil, ¼ teaspoon salt, and garlic; rub mixture evenly over both sides of lamb. Cover and marinate in refrigerator at least 2 hours or overnight.
2. Prepare grill.
3. Sprinkle both sides of lamb with ¼ teaspoon salt and pepper. Place lamb on a grill rack coated with cooking spray; grill 3 minutes on each side (145° for medium-rare) or until desired degree of doneness. Garnish with rosemary sprigs, if desired. Yield: 4 servings (serving size: 2 chops).

CALORIES 218 (43% from fat); FAT 10.4g (sat 3.5g, mono 4.9g, poly 0.7g); PROTEIN 28.6g; CARB 0.4g; FIBER 0.1g; CHOL 91mg; IRON 2.0mg; SODIUM 316mg; CALC 21mg

Sautéed Button and Porcini Mushrooms

Here's a recipe that showcases the rich flavor of dried wild porcini mushrooms. This robust side dish can hold its own when served with lamb, beef tenderloin, or game.
Baron de Ley "Finca Monasterio" Rioja

1   cup dried porcini mushrooms (about 1 ounce)
1   cup water
1   tablespoon olive oil
2   garlic cloves, minced
2   tablespoons minced fresh flat-leaf parsley
16 ounces button mushrooms, sliced
½   teaspoon salt
¼   teaspoon black pepper

1. Soak porcini mushrooms with 1 cup water in a bowl; cover and let stand for 15 minutes or until softened. Drain mushrooms in a fine sieve over a bowl, reserving liquid.
2. Put oil and garlic in a large skillet over medium-high heat; sauté until garlic sizzles. Add porcinis, reserved mushroom liquid, and parsley; cook until the liquid evaporates. Add button mushrooms, salt, and pepper; cook for 15 minutes or until the liquid has evaporated. Yield: 4 servings (serving size: ¾ cup).

CALORIES 83 (42% from fat); FAT 3.9g (sat 0.6g, mono 2.6g, poly 0.5g); PROTEIN 3.2g; CARB 11.3g; FIBER 2.4g; CHOL 0mg; IRON 1.7mg; SODIUM 299mg; CALC 11mg

Peach-Ginger Crisp

Start with juicy fresh summer peaches, and top them with an almond-brown sugar mixture. The hint of fresh ginger adds another level of flavor to this simple fruit dessert.
Domaine des Baumard Quarts de Chaume

½   cup all-purpose flour
¼   cup granulated sugar
¼   cup packed brown sugar
3   tablespoons chilled butter, cut into small pieces
2   tablespoons sliced almonds, toasted
6   cups peeled sliced peaches (about 3 pounds)
1   tablespoon granulated sugar
2   teaspoons cornstarch
2   teaspoons lemon juice
¾   teaspoon minced peeled fresh ginger

1. Preheat oven to 375°.
2. Lightly spoon flour into a dry measuring cup, and level with a knife. Combine flour, ¼ cup granulated sugar, and brown sugar in a bowl. Cut in butter with a pastry blender or 2 knives until crumbly. Stir in almonds.
3. Combine peaches and remaining 4 ingredients in a bowl. Spoon peach mixture into an 8-inch square baking dish. Sprinkle with flour mixture. Bake at 375° for 45 minutes or until lightly browned and bubbly. Yield: 5 servings (serving size: 1 cup).

CALORIES 300 (26% from fat); FAT 8.6g (sat 4.5g, mono 3g, poly 0.7g); PROTEIN 3.3g; CARB 56g; FIBER 4.6g; CHOL 19mg; IRON 1.2mg; SODIUM 76mg; CALC 30mg

A meal without wine is as a day without sunshine.

—Louis Vaudable, French restaurateur

dinner at dusk

In summer, there's no time more special than twilight: The heat of the day begins to melt away, cold white wine is splashed into glasses, and it's finally cool enough to feel hungry (if not actually ravenous). This menu works best with—in fact, *deserves*—a wine for each course.

menu | wine

Lemon-Shallot Scallops

———

Pecorino Breadsticks

Pork Tenderloin with Nectarine-Apricot Sauce

Herbed Orzo

Green and Yellow Wax Beans with Roasted Pepper

———

Roasted Plums with Ginger and Pecans

Serves 6

Scallops possess a unique flavor—pure, sweet, oceanic, and something else quite indescribable. Whatever the "scallop-ness" of scallops is, it works beautifully with Saint-Véran (sometimes abbreviated as St.-Véran), a dry, lemony chardon-nay from the village of Saint-Vérand in the Burgundy region of France. Saint-Vérans are not oaky, and their crispness—along with a hint of minerals and vanilla—is beautifully harmonious with the sea-fresh flavor of scallops pan-seared in just a touch of butter and citrus. Some top Saint-Vérans include the name of the vineyard from which the wine comes. I love the sheer intensity of **Roger Lassarat Saint-Véran "Les Chataigniers" Vieilles Vignes** ($$$).

Pork Tenderloin with Nectarine-Apricot Sauce says one thing to me: riesling. Rieslings—especially those from Germany—are so effusively packed with nectarine and apricot flavors that this pairing is an automatic winner. Historically, too, riesling has always been the traditional wine for pork because its bolt of refreshing acidity counterbalances the natural sweetness of the meat. These pan-seared medallions pair perfectly with a German riesling at the *spätlese* level of ripeness. (For more information, see page 97.) A spätlese is not sweet, but it *is* gorgeously fruity. One of my favorites is **Dr. Loosen Ürziger Würzgarten Riesling Spätlese** ($$$), from the Mosel-Saar-Ruwer region of Germany.

And, finally, there are few wine-and-food experiences that can make you totally ecstatic. **Trimbach Gewürztraminer Vendanges Tardives** ($$$$), from Alsace, France, is a full-bodied sweet white with a texture evocative of whipped cream and an explosive flavor reminiscent of orange marmalade, apri-cots, and lychees. It's deservedly pricey, but when served well chilled the wine becomes the quintessential accompaniment for these roasted plums with their exotic flavors.

Roger Lassarat Saint-Véran "Les Chataigniers" Vieilles Vignes

Dr. Loosen Ürziger Würzgarten Riesling Spätlese

Trimbach Gewürztraminer Vendanges Tardives

Lemon-Shallot Scallops

Lemon-Shallot Scallops

Start your meal with these pan-seared scallops in a zesty lemon-butter sauce.

Roger Lassarat Saint-Véran "Les Chataigniers" Vieilles Vignes

2	teaspoons olive oil
1½	pounds sea scallops
½	teaspoon salt
¼	teaspoon black pepper
2	teaspoons butter
3	tablespoons minced shallots
½	teaspoon minced garlic
¼	cup dry white wine
1	tablespoon fresh lemon juice
2	tablespoons finely chopped fresh parsley
3	cups mixed salad greens
2	teaspoons extravirgin olive oil

1. Heat oil in a large nonstick skillet over high heat. Sprinkle scallops with salt and pepper. Add scallops to pan, and sauté 2 minutes on each side. Remove cooked scallops from pan, and keep warm.
2. Melt butter in pan. Add shallots and garlic; sauté 30 seconds. Add wine and juice; cook 1 minute. Return scallops to pan; toss to coat. Remove from heat; sprinkle with parsley. Place greens in a bowl, and toss with olive oil. Serve scallops over mixed greens. Yield: 6 servings (serving size: 4 ounces scallops and ½ cup greens).

CALORIES 150 (32% from fat); FAT 5.4g (sat 1.3g, mono 2.8g, poly 0.7g); PROTEIN 19.6g; CARB 5.0g; FIBER 0.7g; CHOL 41mg; IRON 0.8mg; SODIUM 393mg; CALC 42mg

Pecorino Breadsticks

Romano cheese takes its name from the city of Rome, and one of the best known types of Romano cheese is sharp and tangy pecorino. This sheep's milk cheese adds a new level of flavor to plain breadsticks.

Roger Lassarat Saint-Véran "Les Chataigniers" Vieilles Vignes

1	package dry yeast (about 2¼ teaspoons)
1⅓	cups warm water (100° to 110°)
3½	cups bread flour, divided
2	tablespoons extravirgin olive oil
1¾	teaspoons salt
1	cup (4 ounces) grated fresh pecorino Romano cheese, divided
	Cooking spray
2	tablespoons cornmeal

1. Dissolve yeast in warm water in a large bowl; let stand 5 minutes. Lightly spoon flour into dry measuring cups; level with a knife. Add ½ cup flour to yeast mixture, stirring with a whisk. Let stand 30 minutes. Add 3 cups flour, oil, and salt; stir until a soft dough forms. Turn dough out onto a lightly floured surface. Knead until smooth and elastic (about 8 minutes); cover and let rest 10 minutes. Knead in ½ cup cheese; cover and let rest 5 minutes. Knead in ½ cup cheese.
2. Place dough in a large bowl coated with cooking spray, turning to coat top. Cover and let rise in a warm place (85°), free from drafts, 45 minutes or until doubled in size. (Gently press two fingers into dough. If indentation remains, dough has risen enough.) Punch dough down. Roll dough into a 12 x 8-inch rectangle on a lightly floured surface.
3. Preheat oven to 450°.
4. Sprinkle 1 tablespoon cornmeal onto each of 2 baking sheets. Cut dough in

Pecorino Breadsticks

half lengthwise to form 2 (12 x 4-inch) rectangles. Cut each rectangle crosswise into 12 (1-inch-wide) strips. Working with 1 dough strip at a time (cover remaining dough to prevent drying), gently roll each strip into a 15-inch-long rope. Place 12 ropes on each prepared pan. Cover and let rise 20 minutes.
5. Uncover dough; bake at 450° for 12 minutes. Remove breadsticks from pans; cool completely on wire racks. Yield: 24 servings (serving size: 1 breadstick).

CALORIES 99 (22% from fat); FAT 2.4g (sat 1.0g, mono 1.2g, poly 0.1g); PROTEIN 4.4g; CARB 15.7g; FIBER 0.7g; CHOL 5mg; IRON 1.1mg; SODIUM 228mg; CALC 52mg

Pork Tenderloin with Nectarine-Apricot Sauce, Herbed Orzo, Green and Yellow Wax Beans with Roasted Pepper

Pork Tenderloin with Nectarine-Apricot Sauce

Simply seasoned pork tenderloin is enhanced with a sweet-and-zesty fruit sauce.

Dr. Loosen Ürziger Würzgarten Riesling Spätlese

- 2 (¾-pound) pork tenderloins, trimmed
- 1 teaspoon salt
- ½ teaspoon freshly ground black pepper
- 2 cups chopped peeled nectarines or peaches
- ¼ cup finely chopped red onion
- ¼ cup finely chopped dried apricots
- 1 tablespoon chopped fresh cilantro
- 1 tablespoon fresh lemon juice
- 1 tablespoon balsamic vinegar
- 1 tablespoon peach nectar
- 1 jalapeño pepper, seeded and finely chopped
- 2 teaspoons olive oil

1. Cut each tenderloin crosswise into 6 pieces. Place plastic wrap over pork; pound to an even thickness (about ¼ inch) using a meat mallet or rolling pin. Sprinkle evenly with salt and pepper.

2. Combine chopped nectarines and next 7 ingredients in a small bowl.

3. Heat oil in a large nonstick skillet over medium-high heat. Add half of pork; cook 3 minutes on each side or until done. Remove from pan; repeat procedure with remaining pork. Serve with nectarine sauce. Yield: 6 servings (serving size: 2 pork medallions and ⅓ cup sauce).

CALORIES 215 (33% from fat); FAT 7.8g (sat 2.3g, mono 3.9g, poly 0.9g); PROTEIN 24.2g; CARB 11.4g; FIBER 1.4g; CHOL 75mg; IRON 1.9mg; SODIUM 450mg; CALC 15mg

Herbed Orzo

The toasted pine nuts add a subtle hint of sweetness to this lemony herbed pasta.

Dr. Loosen Ürziger Würzgarten Riesling Spätlese

- 4 cups hot cooked orzo (about 2 cups uncooked rice-shaped pasta)
- ¼ cup chopped fresh parsley
- 1½ tablespoons fresh lemon juice
- ½ teaspoon chopped fresh oregano
- ¼ teaspoon salt
- ⅛ teaspoon freshly ground black pepper
- 2 tablespoons pine nuts, toasted

1. Cook orzo according to package directions, omitting salt and fat.

2. Combine orzo and next 5 ingredients in a large bowl, and stir well. Top with pine nuts. Yield: 6 servings (serving size: about ⅔ cup).

CALORIES 241 (10% from fat); FAT 2.8g (sat 0.4g, mono 0.5g, poly 1.0g); PROTEIN 8.7g; CARB 45.9g; FIBER 2.1g; CHOL 0mg; IRON 2.3mg; SODIUM 116mg; CALC 16mg

about the wine

Top German wines are organized and labeled according to how ripe the grapes were when they were harvested. Here are the categories you'll find.

Kabinett: A light-bodied wine that's low in alcohol and usually dry. Kabinetts are made from grapes picked during the normal harvest. German wine lovers typically drink them as casual dinner wines.

Spätlese: Literally means "late harvest." Spätleses are made from late-picked, fully ripened grapes. They have greater fruit intensity and strength than kabinett wines. A spätlese may be dry or have a touch of sweetness.

Auslese: Wines made from very ripe grapes harvested in select bunches. Another step upward in richness and intensity. Most ausleses are lush, with some sweetness.

Beerenauslese: BA for short, is a rare and costly sweet wine made from individual grapes selected by hand. Beerenausleses have a deep honeyed richness.

Trockenbeerenauslese: Known as TBA, is the richest, sweetest, rarest, most intense, and most expensive of all German wines. TBAs are produced only in exceptional harvest years and are made from individual grapes shriveled almost to raisins.

entertaining tip

Place a single daisy (with most of its stem removed) in a votive holder or other small container for a simple and festive table decoration. Light up the table by placing unscented white votive candles in an assortment of colored glasses. Colored candles are usually scented and, therefore, interfere with wine tasting.

Green and Yellow Wax Beans with Roasted Pepper

Although it's prettier with the different colors of peppers and beans, this recipe works just fine with one color of each. Take your pick!
Dr. Loosen Ürziger Würzgarten Riesling Spätlese

  1 yellow bell pepper
  1 red bell pepper
  ¾ pound green beans, trimmed
  ¾ pound yellow wax beans, trimmed
  1 teaspoon olive oil
  ½ teaspoon salt
  ¼ teaspoon freshly ground black pepper
  2 teaspoons grated lemon rind
  1 tablespoon fresh lemon juice

1. Preheat broiler.
2. Cut bell peppers in half lengthwise; discard seeds and membranes. Place pepper halves, skin sides up, on a foil-lined baking sheet; flatten with hand. Broil 15 minutes or until blackened. Place in a zip-top plastic bag; seal. Let stand 10 minutes. Peel and cut into thin strips.
3. Place green beans in a large saucepan of boiling water; cook 4 minutes. Remove with a slotted spoon. Plunge beans into ice water; drain. Add wax beans to boiling water; cook 4 minutes. Drain and plunge beans into ice water; drain.
4. Heat oil in a large nonstick skillet over medium-high heat. Add bell pepper strips, beans, salt, and black pepper; sauté 2 minutes or until thoroughly heated. Remove from heat, and add rind and juice, tossing gently to coat. Yield: 6 servings (serving size: 1 cup).

CALORIES 70 (31% from fat); FAT 2.4g (sat 0.4g, mono 1.1g, poly 0.8g); PROTEIN 3.2g; CARB 11.6g; FIBER 4.9g; CHOL 0mg; IRON 1.7mg; SODIUM 203mg; CALC 49mg

Roasted Plums with Ginger and Pecans

The warm plums and syrupy sauce are best served immediately. This dessert is also good with fresh peaches instead of plums.
Trimbach Gewürztraminer Vendanges Tardives

  1 cup sweet gewürztraminer
  ⅓ cup dried apricots, chopped
  3 tablespoons sugar
  1 tablespoon butter, softened
  1 teaspoon grated peeled fresh ginger
  1 large egg yolk, lightly beaten
  3 tablespoons chopped pecans, toasted
  6 red plums, halved and pitted
  ¾ cup vanilla low-fat frozen yogurt
Fresh mint (optional)

1. Preheat oven to 350°.
2. Bring wine to a simmer in a medium saucepan over medium-high heat. Stir in apricots; cover and remove from heat. Let stand 20 minutes. Drain apricots in a colander over a bowl; reserve wine and apricots separately.
3. Combine sugar, butter, ginger, and egg yolk in a bowl. Stir in apricots and pecans. Fill each plum half with 2 teaspoons apricot filling. Place stuffed plums in a single layer in an 11 x 7-inch baking dish; pour reserved wine around plums. Bake at 350° for 20 minutes or until plums are tender.
4. Remove plums from dish; pour remaining liquid into a small saucepan. Bring to a boil; cook until mixture is slightly syrupy and reduced to ¼ cup (about 5 minutes). Serve plum halves with sauce and frozen yogurt. Garnish with mint, if desired. Yield: 6 servings (serving size: 2 plum halves, 2 teaspoons sauce, and 2 tablespoons frozen yogurt).

CALORIES 167 (31% from fat); FAT 5.7g (sat 1.9g, mono 2.4g, poly 1.0g); PROTEIN 2.8g; CARB 28.2g; FIBER 1.8g; CHOL 40mg; IRON 0.9mg; SODIUM 33mg; CALC 53mg

Roasted Plums with
Ginger and Pecans

autumn

Wine is alive, and when you offer it to your
fellow man you are offering him life.
—Clifton Fadiman, American author

For anyone who lives in the country, as I do, autumn is the most enchanting season. The world changes color before our eyes. The garden, in a state of anarchy, looks contentedly spent from its labors. The air, suddenly cool, makes me want to turn on the oven and cook something slowly for hours. It's in autumn that I think vineyards like ours are at their most beautiful. The heavy purple grapes have been harvested. The leaves on the vines are fragile and auburn colored. I walk with our dogs, Lucy and Franny, through the rows, watching as they instinctively find the softest bed of leaves in which to roll, occasionally lying completely upside down, paws in the air. A good vineyard dog knows the

Autumn reminds us why we love food and wine. Autumn is an affirmation.

joy of the harvest. The harvest, of course, is a parable. For seven thousand years, vines clutching the earth have happily thrust themselves upward toward the sun and given us juicy berries—and ultimately wine. And so it is that wine ineluctably connects us to that earth. Wine matters because of this connection. Wine and food are like warm arms that cradle us in our own humanity. It is perhaps no surprise that drinking wine and eating food are the most basic and natural of celebrations. They are the everyday pleasures that carry life forward and sustain us. Autumn reminds us why we love food and wine. Autumn is an affirmation.

autumn light

I love this menu for the way the dishes exude the full, savory flavors of autumn. And yet, absent meat or meat-based stocks, these dishes also possess a lightness that belies their flavor intensities. This menu is at once rich, fruity, sweet, and spicy. What more could one want?

menu | wine

Curried Butternut Squash Soup

Pear-Cheese Strata

Raisin-Rosemary Rye Bread

Spiced Fig and Walnut Bread

Molasses-Spice Cake with Caramel Icing

Serves 10

Winewise, there are two ways to go: When I want a single dry wine to pair with savory dishes (as is often true for lunch or brunch), the hands-down best bet is a California riesling. **Firestone Vineyard Riesling** ($), from California's Central Coast, for example, has just the right body weight to hold its own with this menu's thick soup, as well as with the oozingly opulent custard. Equally important, the riesling's fruitiness—tinged as it is with the merest touch of sweetness—offsets the soup's curry perfectly. That fruitiness also underscores the strata's caramelized pear flavors. And, finally, riesling picks up on the dried fruit sweetness in both breads.

For dinner, I like to serve a progression of wines and dishes. After the riesling paired with the soup, I'll bring out a top-notch chardonnay to go with the strata and bread. Pear and custard flavors in the strata are excellent with chardonnay, which mirrors those tastes. Chardonnay is also superb with figs, nuts, and such baking spices as nutmeg, so the Spiced Fig and Walnut Bread in particular is delicious served here. Be sure the chardonnay you choose isn't too oaky. A favorite of mine is **Silverado Vineyards Chardonnay** ($$), from California's Napa Valley.

With a traditional spice cake, I love to serve Hungarian Tokaji Aszú, considered for centuries to be one of the most legendary and exquisitely refined dessert wines in the world. The spice cake's discreet spiciness and mellow earthy sweetness (from a hint of brown sugar and molasses) is magnificent with the **Royal Tokaji Wine Company Tokaji Aszú 5 Puttonyos** ($$$ for a 500-milliliter bottle), with its melt-in-your-mouth flavors of honey, vanilla, orange marmalade, and caramel.

Firestone Vineyard Riesling

Silverado Vineyards Chardonnay

Royal Tokaji Wine Company Tokaji Aszú 5 Puttonyos

Curried Butternut Squash Soup

Curried Butternut Squash Soup

Curry, cumin, and red pepper add a kick to this creamy squash and apple soup.

Firestone Vineyard Riesling

- 2 teaspoons vegetable oil
- 1 cup thinly sliced leek (about 1 large)
- 1 tablespoon curry powder
- 1 tablespoon brown sugar
- 3/4 teaspoon ground cumin
- 1/4 teaspoon ground red pepper
- 5 garlic cloves, chopped
- 6 cups chopped peeled butternut squash (about 3 pounds)
- 6 cups water
- 4 cups chopped peeled Granny Smith apple (about 1 pound)
- 1/3 cup whipping cream
- 3/4 teaspoon salt
- 2/3 cup minced fresh cilantro

1. Heat oil in a large Dutch oven over medium heat. Add leek and next 5 ingredients; cook 2 minutes, stirring frequently. Add squash, water, and apple; bring to a boil. Cover, reduce heat, and simmer 25 minutes or until tender.

2. Place half of soup in a blender, and process until smooth. Pour pureed soup into a large bowl. Repeat procedure with remaining soup. Return soup to pan; stir in cream and salt. Cook 1 minute or until thoroughly heated. Sprinkle each serving with about 1 tablespoon cilantro. Yield: 10 servings (serving size: 1 cup).

CALORIES 139 (28% from fat); FAT 4.3g (sat 2.0g, mono 1.1g, poly 0.8g); PROTEIN 2.0g; CARB 26.5g; FIBER 6.0g; CHOL 11mg; IRON 1.5mg; SODIUM 188mg; CALC 87mg

Pear-Cheese Strata

The nutty flavor of Gouda cheese balances the sweetness of the pears in this savory egg-and-cheese bread pudding. *Don't* use a smoked Gouda in this recipe because it changes the flavor entirely.

Firestone Vineyard Riesling or
Silverado Vineyards Chardonnay

   Cooking spray
- 10 (1 3/4-ounce) slices sturdy white bread
- 2 cups late harvest sweet riesling or other sweet white wine
- 1/4 teaspoon salt
- 1/4 teaspoon black pepper
- 1 1/2 cups (6 ounces) young Gouda, shredded
- 3 Bartlett pears, peeled, cored, and cut lengthwise into 1/4-inch-thick slices (about 4 cups)
- 3 cups fat-free milk
- 4 large eggs

1. Coat a 13 x 9-inch baking dish with cooking spray. Arrange 5 bread slices in bottom of dish in a single layer. Pour 1 cup wine over bread. Sprinkle with 1/8 teaspoon salt and 1/8 teaspoon pepper. Top with 3/4 cup cheese. Arrange pear slices over cheese; repeat layers of bread, wine, salt, pepper, and cheese.

2. Combine milk and eggs in a bowl; stir well with a whisk. Pour milk mixture over bread mixture. Let stand 20 minutes.

3. Preheat oven to 425°.

4. Cover strata with foil, and bake at 425° for 30 minutes. Uncover and bake an additional 25 minutes or until golden brown. Let stand 10 minutes. Yield: 10 servings (serving size: 1/10 of strata).

CALORIES 319 (30% from fat); FAT 10.6g (sat 4.0g, mono 3.3g, poly 0.6g); PROTEIN 13.0g; CARB 40.6g; FIBER 1.6g; CHOL 102mg; IRON 2.2mg; SODIUM 701mg; CALC 264mg

Pear-Cheese Strata

Raisin-Rosemary Rye Bread

Raisin-Rosemary Rye Bread

Because rye flour produces a soft dough, this recipe also has whole wheat flour, bread flour, and cornmeal to give the loaf body.

**Firestone Vineyard Riesling or
Silverado Vineyards Chardonnay**

1	tablespoon sugar
1	package dry yeast (about 2¼ teaspoons)
1½	cups warm water (100° to 110°)
1	teaspoon olive oil
2⅓	cups bread flour, divided
1	cup whole wheat flour
½	cup rye flour
⅓	cup nonfat dry milk
¼	cup yellow cornmeal
1	teaspoon salt
¾	teaspoon coarsely ground black pepper
1	cup raisins
½	cup chopped walnuts
1½	tablespoons dried rosemary
	Cooking spray

1. Dissolve sugar and yeast in warm water in a large bowl; let stand 5 minutes. Stir in oil. Lightly spoon flours into dry measuring cups; level with a knife. Combine 2 cups bread flour, whole wheat flour, and next 5 ingredients in a bowl. Add flour mixture to yeast mixture. Turn dough out onto a lightly floured surface. Knead until smooth and elastic (about 10 minutes); add enough of remaining bread flour, 1 tablespoon at a time, to prevent dough from sticking to hands. Knead in raisins, walnuts, and rosemary.

2. Place dough in a large bowl coated with cooking spray, turning to coat top. Cover and let rise in a warm place (85°), free from drafts, 45 minutes or until doubled in size. (Gently press two fingers into dough. If indentation remains, dough has risen enough.) Punch dough down; cover and let rest 10 minutes. Form dough into a ball; place in a 9-inch pie plate coated with cooking spray. Cover and let rise 30 minutes or until doubled in size.

3. Preheat oven to 400°.

4. Uncover dough. Score top of loaf in a diamond pattern using a sharp knife. Bake at 400° for 50 minutes or until loaf sounds hollow when tapped. Remove from pan, and cool on a wire rack.

5. To serve bread, cut loaf in half crosswise. Place cut sides down, and cut each half into slices. Yield: 20 servings (serving size: 1 slice).

CALORIES 149 (16% from fat); FAT 2.6g (sat 0.3g, mono 0.6g, poly 1.4g); PROTEIN 5.0g; CARB 27.7g; FIBER 1.9g; CHOL 0mg; IRON 1.5mg; SODIUM 130mg; CALC 39mg

Spiced Fig and Walnut Bread

Try this bread with a bite of goat cheese topped with fig preserves.

**Firestone Vineyard Riesling or
Silverado Vineyards Chardonnay**

2	cups all-purpose flour
¾	cup sugar
1½	teaspoons baking powder
1½	teaspoons ground cinnamon
1	teaspoon ground ginger
½	teaspoon baking soda
½	teaspoon salt
½	teaspoon ground allspice
¼	teaspoon ground nutmeg
½	cup chopped walnuts
8	dried dark-skinned fresh figs, chopped (such as Black Mission)
1	cup low-fat buttermilk
⅓	cup molasses
2	tablespoons vegetable oil
2	large eggs
	Cooking spray

1. Preheat oven to 350°.

2. Lightly spoon flour into dry measuring cups; level with a knife. Combine flour, sugar, and next 7 ingredients in a large bowl; make a well in center of mixture. Stir in walnuts and figs. Combine buttermilk, molasses, vegetable oil, and eggs in a medium bowl; add to flour mixture. Stir mixture just until moist.

3. Spoon batter into an 8 x 4-inch loaf pan coated with cooking spray. Bake at 350° for 1 hour or until a wooden pick inserted in center comes out clean. Cool 10 minutes in pan on a wire rack; remove from pan. Cool completely on wire rack. Yield: 12 servings (serving size: 1 slice).

CALORIES 246 (25% from fat); FAT 6.8g (sat 1.2g, mono 1.8g, poly 3.4g); PROTEIN 5.5g; CARB 42.2g; FIBER 2.0g; CHOL 37mg; IRON 2.1mg; SODIUM 238mg; CALC 104mg

entertaining tip

Set a harvest table outdoors in the crisp fall air, and use fresh squash, pears, and apples as decorative accents.

> No meal is ever dull when there is wine to
> drink and talk about.
>
> —André Simon, French wine authority

about the wine

Tokaji Aszú (pronounced Toe-KIGH-
AZOO), historically called *vinum regum,
rex vinorum*—meaning "the wine of kings,
the king of wines"—is the sublimely
delicious result of furmint, hárslevelü,
and muscat lunel grapes that have been
attacked by the fungus *Botrytis cinerea*,
which concentrates the sweet juice in the
grapes and makes such wines as this
(and French Sauternes) possible. The
sweetness of a Tokaji is measured in
what are called *puttonyos*, ranging
from three (the least sweet) to six (the
sweetest). The number of puttonyos is
listed on the wine label.

Molasses-Spice Cake
with Caramel Icing

The comforting aromas of allspice, cinnamon,
and cloves waft through your kitchen as you
bake this old-fashioned spice cake. The rich
caramel icing is as golden as the season.
**Royal Tokaji Wine Company Tokaji Aszú
5 Puttonyos**

CAKE:

Cooking spray
 1 tablespoon all-purpose flour
 1 cup sugar
 ⅓ cup vegetable shortening
 1 teaspoon vanilla extract
 3 large eggs
1¾ cups all-purpose flour
1½ teaspoons baking powder
 1 teaspoon ground cinnamon
 ½ teaspoon salt
 ¼ teaspoon ground allspice
 ¼ teaspoon ground cloves
 ¾ cup 1% low-fat milk
 ¼ cup molasses

ICING:

 1 cup packed dark brown sugar
 ½ cup 1% low-fat milk
 2 tablespoons butter
 ¼ teaspoon salt
1½ cups sifted powdered sugar
 ½ teaspoon vanilla extract
 ¼ cup chopped pecans, toasted

1. Preheat oven to 350°.

2. Coat bottoms of 2 (8-inch) round cake
pans with cooking spray (do not coat sides
of pans); line bottoms with wax paper.
Coat wax paper with cooking spray; dust
with 1 tablespoon flour.

3. To prepare cake, beat sugar, shortening,
and vanilla with a mixer at medium speed
for 5 minutes. Add eggs, 1 at a time, beating well after each addition. Lightly spoon
1¾ cups flour into dry measuring cups;
level with a knife. Combine 1¾ cups flour
and next 5 ingredients in a large bowl,
stirring well with a whisk. Combine milk
and molasses. Add flour mixture to sugar
mixture alternately with milk mixture,
beginning and ending with flour mixture.

4. Pour batter into prepared pans. Sharply
tap pans once on counter to remove air
bubbles. Bake at 350° for 23 to 25 minutes
or until a wooden pick inserted in center
comes out clean. Cool in pans 10 minutes
on a wire rack; remove from pans. Remove
wax paper. Cool completely on wire rack.

5. To prepare icing, combine 1 cup brown
sugar, ½ cup milk, 2 tablespoons butter,
and ¼ teaspoon salt in a medium
saucepan. Bring to a boil over medium-
high heat, stirring constantly. Reduce
heat, and simmer until slightly thick
(about 5 minutes), stirring occasionally.
Remove from heat. Add powdered sugar
and ½ teaspoon vanilla; beat with a mixer
at medium speed 9 minutes or until icing is
smooth and only slightly warm. (Icing will
continue to thicken as it cools.)

6. Place 1 cake layer on a serving platter.
Working quickly, spread layer with half of
icing, and top with remaining layer.
Spread remaining icing over top layer, and
sprinkle with toasted pecans. Cool to
room temperature. Store cake loosely
covered in refrigerator. Yield: 18 servings
(serving size: 1 slice).

CALORIES 257 (25% from fat); FAT 7.2g (sat 2.2g, mono 2.6g, poly 1.5g);
PROTEIN 3.1g; CARB 45.8g; FIBER 0.6g; CHOL 39mg; IRON 1.3mg;
SODIUM 173mg; CALC 73mg

Sun-Dried Tomato Meat Loaf
with Red Currant-Beaujolais Sauce

homestyle supper

When autumn air takes on that unmistakable chill, there's nothing more comforting than dining on helpings of meat loaf and mashed potatoes, along with a glass of good red wine.

menu | wine

Sun-Dried Tomato Meat Loaf with Red Currant-Beaujolais Sauce

Classic Mashed Potatoes

Whole wheat dinner rolls

———

Pear-Cranberry Crisp

Serves 5

This main course is not your mother's meat loaf—at least it's not *my* mother's meat loaf. The trio of sun-dried tomatoes, fresh basil, and grated Parmigiano-Reggiano cheese pulls the flavor of this meat loaf in a decidedly more delicious direction. But what I may love the most about this dish is the way the red currant-Beaujolais sauce underscores the meat loaf's satisfying meaty flavors and steers away from the sticky sweetness of ketchup. However, no matter how upscale this meat loaf tastes it's still meat loaf, so pairing it with a pricey wine just wouldn't feel right. Meat loaf and mashed potatoes call for a wine that's gratifying, lip-smacking, and in every possible way just plain good—but it should also be humble.

Beaujolais is the perfect choice. Made from gamay grapes, Beaujolais, bursting with wild berry and cherry flavors, is a favorite "everyday wine" in bistros all over France. There are three ascending quality levels: basic Beaujolais, Beaujolais-Villages, and Beaujolais Cru. A Beaujolais Cru works best here because its more vivid berry flavors balance the full-flavored meat loaf and harmonize with the red currant jelly. My favorite is **Georges Duboeuf Fleurie "Domaine des Quatre Vents"** ($). Serve this with a slight chill to pump up the fruity flavors; putting the bottle in the fridge 15 minutes before opening will do the trick.

There's a must-have wine that's so delicious with the Pear-Cranberry Crisp that you shouldn't miss it: **Quady "Elysium"** ($ for a 375-milliliter half bottle), from California. Made from black muscat grapes, Elysium has a red fruit, rose petal character that's exactly on the mark with such high-toned fruits as cranberries. At the same time, the wine's luscious spiciness works well in juxtaposition to the crisp's sweet pear and maple syrup flavors. The name *Elysium* is Greek for heaven—which describes this match perfectly.

Georges Duboeuf Fleurie "Domaine des Quatre Vents"

Quady "Elysium"

about the wine

The best Beaujolais are named after 10 special villages (the so-called *cru*): St.-Amour, Juliénas, Chénas, Moulin-à-Vent, Fleurie, Chiroubles, Morgon, Régnié, Brouilly, and Côte de Brouilly.

Sun-Dried Tomato Meat Loaf with Red Currant-Beaujolais Sauce

Red currant jelly and Beaujolais make a quick, rich sauce that is a sophisticated change from the typical ketchup topping.
Georges Duboeuf Fleurie "Domaine des Quatre Vents" (Beaujolais)

MEAT LOAF:
  Cooking spray
1½ (1-ounce) slices white bread
1¼ pounds ground round
  ½ cup finely chopped onion
  ½ cup (2 ounces) grated fresh Parmigiano-Reggiano cheese
  ¼ cup thinly sliced fresh basil
2½ tablespoons sun-dried tomato sprinkles
  2 tablespoons chopped fresh parsley
  ¼ teaspoon salt
  ⅛ teaspoon pepper
  2 garlic cloves, minced
  1 large egg, lightly beaten
SAUCE:
  ¼ cup red currant jelly
  2 tablespoons Beaujolais
  ½ teaspoon all-purpose flour

1. Preheat oven to 400°.
2. Coat an 8 x 4-inch loaf pan with cooking spray; set aside.
3. To prepare meat loaf, place bread in a food processor; pulse 10 times or until coarse crumbs form. Combine crumbs, meat, and next 9 ingredients in a bowl. Press meat mixture into prepared pan.
4. Bake at 400° for 55 minutes or until a meat thermometer registers 160°.
5. To prepare sauce, combine jelly, wine, and flour in a small saucepan. Bring to a boil; cook 5 minutes or until jelly melts. Serve with meat loaf. Yield: 5 servings (serving size: 5 ounces meat loaf and about 1 tablespoon sauce).

CALORIES 313 (33% from fat); FAT 11.6g (sat 4.9g, mono 4.3g, poly 0.6g); PROTEIN 33.0g; CARB 18.5g; FIBER 0.8g; CHOL 115mg; IRON 3.2mg; SODIUM 477mg; CALC 173mg

Classic Mashed Potatoes

Creamy and buttery mashed potatoes are the perfect partner for meat loaf.
Georges Duboeuf Fleurie "Domaine des Quatre Vents" (Beaujolais)

1½ pounds cubed peeled baking potato
  ¼ cup 2% reduced-fat milk
  ¼ cup fat-free, less-sodium chicken broth
1½ tablespoons light sour cream
  ½ teaspoon salt
  ¼ teaspoon pepper
  2 tablespoons butter, softened

1. Place potato in a large saucepan, and cover with water. Bring to a boil. Reduce heat; simmer 15 minutes or until potato is tender.
2. Drain and return potato to pan. Add milk and broth; mash to desired consistency. Cook 2 minutes or until potato is thoroughly heated, stirring constantly. Stir in sour cream, salt, and pepper. Top with butter. Yield: 5 servings (serving size: about ⅔ cup).

CALORIES 154 (30% from fat); FAT 5.2g (sat 3.3g, mono 1.3g, poly 0.2g); PROTEIN 2.9g; CARB 24.7g; FIBER 2.1g; CHOL 14mg; IRON 0.4mg; SODIUM 312mg; CALC 22mg

Pear-Cranberry Crisp

A crisp is a classic wholesome American fall dessert that's easier to make than a pie but creates the same warming mood.
Quady "Elysium"

FILLING:
  6 cups sliced peeled ripe Bartlett pear (about 3 pounds)
  1 teaspoon cornstarch
  ½ cup fresh cranberries
  ½ cup apple juice
  ¼ cup maple syrup
  1 teaspoon vanilla extract
  ¾ teaspoon ground ginger
  ⅛ teaspoon sea salt
  Cooking spray
TOPPING:
  ¾ cup regular oats
  ¾ cup whole wheat pastry flour
  ¼ cup sugar
  ¼ cup chopped pecans
  ¼ cup butter, melted
  1 teaspoon vanilla extract
  ¼ teaspoon sea salt

1. Preheat oven to 375°.
2. To prepare filling, place pear in a large bowl. Sprinkle with cornstarch; toss well to coat. Stir in cranberries and next 5 ingredients. Spoon pear mixture into a 2-quart baking dish coated with cooking spray.
3. To prepare topping, combine oats and remaining 6 ingredients, tossing until moist. Sprinkle topping in an even layer over pear mixture. Cover with foil; bake at 375° for 40 minutes. Uncover and bake an additional 20 minutes or until topping is golden and fruit mixture is bubbly. Yield: 8 servings (serving size: about ¾ cup).

CALORIES 310 (30% from fat); FAT 10.2g (sat 3.9g, mono 3.4g, poly 1.3g); PROTEIN 4.2g; CARB 55.4g; FIBER 4.8g; CHOL 15mg; IRON 1.1mg; SODIUM 168mg; CALC 40mg

Pear-Cranberry Crisp

Singapore Mai Fun

asian-style dinner

Asian flavors feel right at home in any season. But the warming character of soup and the comforting satisfaction of noodles seem especially delicious in autumn. I wouldn't dream of having any of these simply delicious dishes (including the Ginger Pudding) without an equally delicious wine alongside.

menu | wine

Hot-and-Sour Coconut Soup

Singapore Mai Fun

Ginger Pudding

Serves 6

In a typical Asian-inspired dish, the flavors aren't so much melded as they are poised in dramatic opposition: Lime is juxtaposed against sugar, which in turn counterbalances chile paste ... pungent ginger and snappy lemongrass offset the creaminess of coconut milk ... and so on. Therefore, an accompanying wine needs to be bold enough to handle flavors that are exploding in all directions.

Then there's what I call the "clean flavor" factor. Lemongrass, lime, and ginger have bracingly clean, precise flavors, which rarely work with a wine that has been made and aged in oak (such as most chardonnays). Often buttery on the palate, oaky wines taste out of whack next to the precision that, say, ginger possesses.

What *does* work brilliantly—and is my favorite wine for Hot-and-Sour Coconut Soup and Singapore Mai Fun—is an out-rageously vivid, lush, spicy gewürztraminer. (Gewürztraminers are never made using oak.) **Gundlach Bundschu "Rhinefarm Vineyard" Gewürztraminer** ($$), from the Sonoma Valley of California, leaps with the aromas and flavors of rose petals, spices, gingerbread, and lychees.

Lively and soothing at the same time, Ginger Pudding is a captivating end to this meal, especially if you accompany it with a glass of **Washington Hills Late Harvest Riesling** ($), from the Columbia Valley of Washington State. This wine is seductively sweet but not sugary, and has just the right pure peach, apricot, and exotic fruit flavors to heighten the enjoyment of the pudding. Pudding, of course, has an overt melt-in-your-mouth creaminess that virtually demands a wine with natural underlying acidity to provide contrast—and riesling is the wine for the job.

*Gundlach Bundschu
"Rhinefarm Vineyard"
Gewürztraminer*

*Washington Hills
Late Harvest Riesling*

Hot-and-Sour Coconut Soup

Infuse a simple base of chicken broth with the authentic Thai flavors of ginger, cilantro, garlic, and lemongrass—and fresh basil is a must.

Gundlach Bundschu "Rhinefarm Vineyard" Gewürztraminer

¼ cup (1-inch-thick) slices peeled fresh ginger

¼ cup chopped fresh cilantro

3 garlic cloves, halved

2 (10-inch) stalks fresh lemongrass, each cut into 2-inch pieces

2 (14-ounce) cans fat-free, less-sodium chicken broth

Cooking spray

8 ounces skinless, boneless chicken breast halves

8 ounces fresh sliced mushrooms

1 cup light coconut milk

1 tablespoon Thai fish sauce

2 teaspoons ground fresh chile paste with garlic (such as sambal oelek)

1 cup snow peas, halved crosswise

⅓ cup chopped fresh basil

2 tablespoons fresh lime juice

1. Place first 5 ingredients in a large saucepan; bring to a boil. Cover, reduce heat, and simmer 20 minutes. Strain mixture through a sieve into a bowl; discard solids. Return infused broth to pan.

2. Heat a large nonstick skillet over medium-high heat; coat with cooking spray, and add chicken. Cook 4 minutes on each side or until lightly browned. Remove from pan. Add mushrooms to pan; sauté 5 minutes or until tender.

3. Cut chicken into bite-sized pieces. Add chicken, mushrooms, coconut milk, fish sauce, and chile paste to broth in saucepan; bring to a boil. Reduce heat, and simmer 10 minutes. Add peas; cook 3 minutes. Remove from heat; stir in basil and lime juice. Yield: 6 servings (serving size: about 1 cup).

NOTE: To use the lemongrass, discard the tough outer leaves and use the lower bulbous portion of the stem. Slice or chop according to recipe directions.

CALORIES 101 (26% from fat); FAT 2.9g (sat 1.5g, mono 0.2g, poly 0.3g); PROTEIN 12.9g; CARB 5.9g; FIBER 1.7g; CHOL 22mg; IRON 1.5mg; SODIUM 742mg; CALC 17mg

Singapore Mai Fun

This curried noodle dish is a sure hit and ready in a snap—if you have the ingredients prepped beforehand. You'll find skinny rice noodles in the supermarket's ethnic foods section.

Gundlach Bundschu "Rhinefarm Vineyard" Gewürztraminer

1 (6-ounce) package skinny rice stick noodles (*py mai fun*)
½ cup fat-free, less-sodium chicken broth
3 tablespoons low-sodium soy sauce
1 teaspoon sugar
½ teaspoon salt
Cooking spray
1 tablespoon peanut oil, divided
1 large egg, lightly beaten
½ cup thin red bell pepper strips
1 tablespoon grated peeled fresh ginger
¼ teaspoon crushed red pepper
3 garlic cloves, minced
8 ounces skinless, boneless chicken breast, thinly sliced
1 tablespoon hot curry powder
8 ounces medium shrimp, peeled and deveined
½ teaspoon fresh lime juice
½ cup (1-inch) slices green onions

1. Cook rice noodles according to package directions. Drain.
2. Combine broth, soy sauce, sugar, and salt; stir until sugar dissolves.
3. Heat a large nonstick skillet or wok over medium-high heat; coat pan with cooking spray. Add 1 teaspoon oil. Add egg; stir-fry 30 seconds or until soft-scrambled, stirring constantly. Remove from pan. Wipe pan clean with a paper towel. Heat 2 teaspoons oil in pan over medium-high heat. Add bell pepper strips, ginger, crushed red pepper, and garlic, and stir-fry 15 seconds. Add chicken; stir-fry 2 minutes. Add curry and shrimp; stir-fry 2 minutes. Stir in noodles, broth mixture, and egg; cook 1 minute or until thoroughly heated. Toss with lime juice, and sprinkle with green onions. Yield: 6 servings (serving size: 1 cup).

CALORIES 237 (17% from fat); FAT 4.6g (sat 1.0g, mono 1.7g, poly 1.3g); PROTEIN 19.7g; CARB 27.8g; FIBER 1.3g; CHOL 115mg; IRON 2.2mg; SODIUM 646mg; CALC 53mg

Ginger Pudding

Garnish with a few fresh berries for a contrast in color, texture, and flavor.

Washington Hills Late Harvest Riesling

3 cups 1% low-fat milk, divided
⅓ cup finely chopped crystallized ginger
⅔ cup sugar
3 tablespoons cornstarch
Dash of salt
3 large egg yolks
1 tablespoon butter
1 teaspoon grated lemon rind
1 teaspoon vanilla extract

1. Combine 2½ cups milk and crystallized ginger in a medium saucepan; bring to a simmer over medium heat, stirring frequently. Remove from heat; let stand 5 minutes.
2. Combine ½ cup milk, sugar, cornstarch, salt, and egg yolks in a medium bowl, and stir with a whisk until well blended. Gradually stir one-fourth of hot milk mixture into egg mixture; add to remaining milk mixture, stirring constantly. Bring to a boil over medium heat; cook 1 minute or until thick and creamy, stirring constantly. Remove mixture from heat; stir in butter, rind, and vanilla. Pour into a bowl; cover surface of pudding with plastic wrap. Chill. Yield: 6 servings (serving size: ½ cup).

CALORIES 226 (23% from fat); FAT 5.8g (sat 2.8g, mono 1.9g, poly 0.5g); PROTEIN 5.5g; CARB 38.1g; FIBER 0.1g; CHOL 119mg; IRON 1.9mg; SODIUM 114mg; CALC 179mg

wine tip

Here's an easy pairing principle to remember: Dishes with highly aromatic ingredients—such as ginger, lemongrass, chile paste, fish sauce, curry powder, cilantro, and lime—often taste best served with wines that are also highly aromatic. The four top aromatic wine varietals are gewürztraminer, riesling, muscat, and viognier.

casual harvest dinner

Salad, stew, and the perfect wine. Does a meal get any better than that on an autumn evening? I don't think so. Unless, of course, you have *two* perfect wines!

menu | wine

Classic Caesar Salad

Hunter's Stew

Baguettes

Serves 12

We've all heard the notion that wine and salad don't work together. That's crazy! Every European cuisine, from French to Greek, boasts numerous salads—and Europeans drink more wine than any other people in the world. Still, when I sat at the kitchen table to taste-test Classic Caesar Salad with about a dozen different wines, I have to admit that I braced myself. Anchovy paste ... garlic ... Worcestershire sauce. *Could any wine stand up to that trilogy,* I wondered.

As it turns out, Caesar salad is sensational with certain white wines—especially if they're medium in body and not oaky. A bold gewürztraminer, for example, is a fascinating partner with a Caesar. I also love to pair it with a pinot gris from California, Oregon, or the Alsace region of France. The most accessible partner of all, however, is a crisp but mellow (and not outrageously green) sauvignon blanc. The fresh melony citrus flavors of **Ehlers Estate Sauvignon Blanc** ($$), from the Napa Valley, are a perfect juxtaposition for the sassy, tart, piquant kick of the Caesar salad.

The homeyness of Hunter's Stew requires a different wine— something rustic, comforting, and earthy to pick up on the savory flavors of slow-cooked duck, sausage, and beans. My favorite is Côtes-du-Rhône, a superpopular red in French bistros because it's inexpensive (priced well to partner with stew) and easy to drink. Made mostly from a blend of grenache, mourvèdre, syrah, and carignan, Côtes-du-Rhône often has flavors that subtly suggest beef broth and bacon—a plus given the ingredients in this stew. Côtes-du-Rhône wines come from the southern Rhône Valley of France, in an area surrounding the ancient walled city of Avignon. Try **Château du Trignon Rasteau Côtes-du-Rhône Villages** ($$)—and buy an extra bottle to use in the stew itself.

*Ehlers Estate
Sauvignon Blanc*

*Château du Trignon Rasteau
Côtes-du-Rhône Villages*

Classic Caesar Salad

The Crisp Croutons do double duty: accenting the stew *and* the salad.

Ehlers Estate Sauvignon Blanc

¼ cup egg substitute
1 tablespoon fresh lemon juice
3 tablespoons extravirgin olive oil
3 tablespoons balsamic vinegar
1½ teaspoons anchovy paste
1 teaspoon Worcestershire sauce
½ teaspoon freshly ground black pepper
¼ teaspoon fine sea salt
2 garlic cloves, minced
18 cups torn romaine and hearty field greens
2 cups Crisp Croutons (see recipe below)
¼ cup (1 ounce) grated fresh Parmesan cheese

1. Combine egg substitute and juice; gradually add oil, whisking constantly. Stir in vinegar and next 5 ingredients. Place greens, croutons, and cheese in a large bowl. Add dressing; toss well to coat. Yield: 12 servings (serving size 1½ cups).

(Totals include Crisp Croutons) CALORIES 75 (48% from fat); FAT 4.4g (sat 0.9g, mono 2.8g, poly 0.5g); PROTEIN 3.0g; CARB 6.0g; FIBER 2.0g; CHOL 2mg; IRON 2mg; SODIUM 210mg; CALC 63mg

CRISP CROUTONS

6 cups (½-inch) cubed French bread (about 6 ounces)
1 tablespoon butter, melted
1 teaspoon paprika
1 teaspoon onion powder

1. Preheat oven to 350°.
2. Combine all ingredients in a jelly-roll pan; toss well. Bake at 350° for 20 minutes or until toasted, turning once. Yield: 6 cups.

CALORIES 24 (26% from fat); FAT 0.7g (sat 0.4g, mono 0.2g, poly 0.1g); PROTEIN 0.7g; CARB 4.0g; FIBER 0.2g; CHOL 1mg; IRON 0.2mg; SODIUM 48mg; CALC 6mg

Hunter's Stew

Showcasing the catch from a duck hunt, this hearty stew also includes beans, root vegetables, and herbs. A splash of balsamic vinegar adds a little zing. If you can make the stew a day ahead, the flavors will meld and become even richer.

Château du Trignon Rasteau Côtes-du-Rhône Villages

1 pound dried navy beans
11 cups water, divided
2½ cups (1-inch) chopped peeled rutabaga or turnip
3 cups (1-inch) cubed red or Yukon gold potato
3 cups quartered cremini or button mushrooms (about ½ pound)
2 cups chopped onion
1 cup chopped carrot
1 cup chopped celery
1 (5¾- to 6¼-pound) dressed domestic duck, fresh or thawed
2 chicken drumsticks (about ¾ pound)
2 chicken thighs (about ¾ pound)
9 ounces sweet turkey Italian sausage
3 cups Côtes-du-Rhône or other dry red wine, divided
½ cup finely chopped fresh flat-leaf parsley
2 tablespoons balsamic vinegar
1½ teaspoons dried summer savory
1½ teaspoons dried thyme
1½ teaspoons salt
1½ teaspoons pepper
1 (14-ounce) can fat-free, less-sodium beef broth
2 cups Crisp Croutons (see recipe at left)
Parsley sprigs (optional)

1. Sort and wash beans, and place in a large Dutch oven. Cover with water to 2 inches above beans, and bring to a boil. Cook 2 minutes. Remove from heat. Cover and let stand 1 hour.

2. Drain beans, and return to pan. Add 8 cups water; bring to a boil. Cover and cook 1 hour or until just slightly firm. Drain and set aside.

3. Place 3 cups water in a large stockpot; bring to a boil. Add rutabaga, and cook 5 minutes. Add potato, mushrooms, onion, carrot, and celery, and return to a boil. Reduce heat; simmer 15 minutes or until vegetables are crisp-tender. Set aside (do not drain).

4. Remove and discard giblets and neck from duck. Rinse duck with cold water; pat dry. Trim excess fat. Cut duck into 8 pieces. Heat a large nonstick skillet over medium-high heat. Add duck pieces; sauté 5 minutes on each side or until well browned. Remove from pan. Add chicken pieces; sauté 5 minutes on each side or until well browned. Remove from pan. Add sausage; sauté 10 minutes, browning on all sides. Remove from pan, and cool. Slice sausage into 24 (¾-inch) pieces.

5. Carefully add ¼ cup wine, scraping pan to loosen browned bits, and add pan drippings to stockpot with vegetables. Add beans, duck, chicken, sausage, 2¾ cups wine, chopped parsley, and next 6 ingredients, and bring to a boil. Reduce heat, and simmer 30 minutes. Cover stew, and chill 8 to 24 hours.

6. Skim solidified fat from surface; discard. Reheat over medium heat, stirring frequently to prevent scorching. Bring to a boil. Reduce heat, and simmer 10 minutes. To serve, top stew with Crisp Croutons; garnish with parsley sprigs, if desired. Yield: 12 servings (serving size: about 2 cups stew, 1 poultry piece, 2 sausage pieces, and about 2 tablespoons Crisp Croutons).

(Totals include Crisp Croutons) CALORIES 548 (27% from fat); FAT 16.1g (sat 5.6g, mono 4.0g, poly 3.0g); PROTEIN 55.0g; CARB 41.0g; FIBER 12.0g; CHOL 195mg; IRON 8mg; SODIUM 659mg; CALC 128mg

Hunter's Stew

Roasted Pork and
Autumn Vegetables

flavors of fall

The aroma of succulent pork loin and fall vegetables roasting slowly together in the oven—is there anything more tantalizing? As the meal cooks, open the wine and savor a glass on its own. A fine white Burgundy is chardonnay at its most magnificent.

menu | wine

Roasted Pork and Autumn Vegetables

Romaine Salad

Crusty whole wheat bread

———

Honey-Apple Crumble with Dried Fruit

Serves 8

The key to great-tasting pork? Pair it with white wine. I'll admit that there are pork dishes that go nicely with certain red wines. But over a lifetime of cooking and concentrating on food and wine, in almost every case, the most spectacular matches with pork have been with white wine.

In particular, pork's sweet meaty "porkiness" needs a white wine boldly framed by acidity. That acidity dances with the pork, cutting through its richness and heightening its flavor at the same time. There are, of course, several whites with prominent acidity; among them, riesling is well known as a traditional pork partner. But for this meal, I've chosen white Burgundy. All white Burgundies are made from only chardonnay grapes. But white Burgundy is different than most other chardonnays in one major respect: It has a lot of acidity. In fact, a good white Burgundy possesses all the creamy, caramel voluptuousness that makes chardonnay so appealing; but at the same time, its inherent crispness makes it perfect for pork. A final plus: White Burgundies have a certain earthiness that's fabulous with roasted root vegetables. For this meal, I like to spring for a top-notch white Burgundy, such as **Louis Latour Puligny-Montrachet "Les Truffières" Premier Cru** ($$$$).

Ready for another wow? Taste the apple crumble with a glass of tawny Port. The dessert's cider and apple flavors, rich nuttiness, and cinnamony crunch are all magnificently magnified by the smooth flavors of a great tawny. Any tawny from Portugal is spectacular, but you might also want to try a tawny from Australia, one of the world's best-kept wine secrets. **Penfolds "Grandfather" Fine Old Liqueur Tawny** ($$$$) is roasted nuts, vanilla, toffee, and caramel taken to a wildly hedonistic level.

*Louis Latour
Puligny-Montrachet
"Les Truffières" Premier Cru*

*Penfolds
"Grandfather"
Fine Old Liqueur Tawny*

Roasted Pork and Autumn Vegetables

Pork and root vegetables develop superdeep flavors when you slowly roast them together. It's fine to use a simple California chardonnay in this recipe—save the more expensive white Burgundy for drinking.

Louis Latour Puligny-Montrachet "Les Truffières" Premier Cru (White Burgundy)

2   fennel bulbs (about 1½ pounds)
2   small onions
1   tablespoon olive oil, divided
4   cups (½-inch) cubed peeled rutabaga
¾   pound small carrots (about 16)
1   (2¼-pound) boneless pork loin roast, trimmed
Cooking spray
2   tablespoons chopped fresh sage
¾   teaspoon kosher salt, divided
¾   teaspoon freshly ground black pepper, divided
¾   cup fat-free, less-sodium chicken broth
½   cup chardonnay
2   teaspoons Dijon mustard

1. Preheat oven to 400°.
2. Trim stalks from fennel; discard. Cut each bulb into 8 wedges. Peel onions, leaving roots intact; cut each onion into 8 wedges.
3. Heat 1½ teaspoons oil in a nonstick skillet over medium-high heat. Add fennel and onion; sauté 8 minutes. Remove from pan. Add 1½ teaspoons oil, rutabaga, and carrots to pan; sauté 7 minutes.
4. Place pork on a rack coated with cooking spray; place rack in a shallow roasting pan. Sprinkle pork with sage, ½ teaspoon salt, and ½ teaspoon pepper. Arrange vegetables around pork; sprinkle with ¼ teaspoon salt and ¼ teaspoon pepper.
5. Bake at 400° for 50 minutes or until thermometer registers 160° (slightly pink). Remove pork and vegetables from pan; cover loosely with foil. Remove rack. Place pan over medium heat; stir in broth, wine, and mustard, scraping pan to loosen browned bits. Bring to a boil; reduce heat, and simmer 4 minutes, stirring occasionally. Serve with pork and vegetables. Yield: 8 servings (serving size: 3 ounces pork, about ⅔ cup vegetables, and 2 tablespoons sauce).

CALORIES 282 (37% from fat); FAT 11.5g (sat 3.6g, mono 5.5g, poly 1.0g); PROTEIN 29.9g; CARB 14.6g; FIBER 4.5g; CHOL 78mg; IRON 2.2mg; SODIUM 359mg; CALC 96mg

Romaine Salad

Accompany the roast with a simply dressed green salad.

Louis Latour Puligny-Montrachet "Les Truffières" Premier Cru (White Burgundy)

2   tablespoons light mayonnaise
1   tablespoon Dijon mustard
2   teaspoons fresh lemon juice
1   teaspoon balsamic vinegar
½   teaspoon Worcestershire sauce
1   garlic clove, minced
8   cups torn romaine lettuce

1. Combine first 6 ingredients in a large bowl, stirring with a whisk. Add 8 cups torn romaine lettuce, tossing gently to coat. Yield: 8 servings (serving size: 1 cup).

CALORIES 24 (55% from fat); FAT 1.4g (sat 0.3g, mono 0.0g, poly 0.1g); PROTEIN 0.7g; CARB 2.5g; FIBER 1.2g; CHOL 1mg; IRON 0.6mg; SODIUM 63mg; CALC 20mg

about the wine

Burgundy labels can be confusing, so always buy white Burgundies at a good wine shop, where the merchant can help you with your selection. Remember that all white Burgundies are made exclusively with chardonnay grapes and that the wines come at three ascending levels of quality and expense: so-called *village* wines, *Premier Cru* wines, and *Grand Cru* wines (the most expensive and rarest of all).

Honey-Apple Crumble with Dried Fruit

In addition to rehydrating the dried apricots and cranberries, the cider deepens the flavor of the apples.

Penfolds "Grandfather" Fine Old Liqueur Tawny

2¼   cups apple cider
⅓   cup finely chopped dried apricots
⅓   cup dried cranberries
⅔   cup nutlike cereal nuggets (such as Grape-Nuts)
¾   cup packed brown sugar, divided
½   cup plus 1 tablespoon all-purpose flour, divided
1½   teaspoons ground cinnamon, divided
¼   cup honey
1   teaspoon vanilla extract
5   large Rome apples (about 2½ pounds), each peeled and cut into 12 wedges
Cooking spray

1. Bring cider to a boil. Remove from heat, and stir in apricots and cranberries. Let stand 20 minutes. Drain dried fruit in a colander over a bowl, reserving cider.
2. Preheat oven to 350°.
3. Combine dried fruit, cereal, ¼ cup sugar, 1 tablespoon flour, and 1 teaspoon cinnamon in a bowl.
4. Combine ½ cup sugar, ½ cup flour, and ½ teaspoon cinnamon in a large bowl. Stir in reserved cider, honey, and vanilla. Add apples, tossing gently to coat. Place apple mixture in a 13 x 9-inch baking dish coated with cooking spray; top with cereal mixture.
5. Bake at 350° for 55 minutes. Yield: 8 servings (serving size: 1 cup).

CALORIES 298 (2% from fat); FAT 0.5g (sat 0.1g, mono 0.1g, poly 0.2g); PROTEIN 2.8g; CARB 73.8g; FIBER 3.2g; CHOL 0mg; IRON 4.1mg; SODIUM 68mg; CALC 36mg

about the wine

Australia has a long history of making opulent tawny Port-style wines that are produced in a similar manner as Portuguese tawny Ports. They're a touch sweeter, however, and are usually made from grenache and syrah grapes rather than Portuguese varieties. Aged 10 to 25 years in wood, these tawnies are absolutely bursting with rich, nutty, toffee, and caramel flavors—perfect to pair with this crumble.

Honey-Apple Crumble
with Dried Fruit

Citrus Chicken Tagine

moroccan nights

Want to wake up your senses? The eggplant dip is a tour de force of garlicky flavor, the chicken dish is bursting with citrus and spices, and the stuffed dates are big-style deliciousness in small-sized bites—and each has a fascinating wine partner.

menu | wine

Roasted Eggplant Dip

Pita bread

Citrus Chicken Tagine

Almond-Stuffed Dates

Serves 4

The first time I made Roasted Eggplant Dip I thought I'd serve it with a delicate white wine, since eggplant is very mild. What I hadn't factored in is that eggplant shrivels as it roasts, thus hugely magnifying the one-two-three punch of paprika, cumin, and garlic in this recipe. The wine I'd selected didn't have a chance! Then I brought out a cold bottle of cava—and the combination was magic. Cava, a Spanish sparkling wine, is more rustic than Champagne. Its lively, unfussy flavor and rabble-rousing bubbles instantly clean and refresh the palate, leaving you raring to go for another bite of the dramatic dip. A favorite that's fabulously priced is **Freixenet "Cordon Negro" Brut Cava** ($), from Spain.

Combining fruits with meat is an ancient Mediterranean idea, and it's the key to this citrusy chicken stew that was inspired by Moroccan tagines. Most stews are slow-cooked for long periods until their flavors meld and mellow. This tagine has a relatively quick cooking time so each flavor stands out singularly and brilliantly. To complement those flavors and balance the acidity, a riesling from Alsace, France, is the perfect choice. Alsace rieslings are fuller in body than rieslings that hail from elsewhere, and their acidity and citrusy peachiness fall right in line with the flavors of this tagine. Among the scores of excellent Alsace rieslings available is **Kuentz-Bas "Pfersigberg" Riesling** ($$$$).

Almonds and such dried fruits as dates are part of the Arabic-influenced cuisine of southern Spain. And both become deliciously hedonistic when accompanied by one of southern Spain's greatest vinous achievements: oloroso Sherry. Orange-tinged mahogany oloroso has sumptuous flavors evocative of roasted nuts, vanilla, and brown sugar. Don't miss **Hidalgo Oloroso Especial Sherry** ($$), from Spain.

Freixenet "Cordon Negro" Brut Cava

Kuentz-Bas "Pfersigberg" Riesling

Hidalgo Oloroso Especial Sherry

Roasted Eggplant Dip

Roasting the eggplant intensifies the flavor
and caramelizes its natural sugars.

Freixenet "Cordon Negro" Brut Cava

  2 (1-pound) eggplants, peeled and cut
      into 1-inch cubes
  ¼ teaspoon salt, divided
  2 tablespoons olive oil, divided
  ¼ teaspoon freshly ground black pepper
Cooking spray
  ¾ cup water
  2 teaspoons paprika
  1 teaspoon ground cumin
  ⅛ teaspoon ground red pepper
  3 garlic cloves, minced
  1 tablespoon chopped fresh flat-leaf
      parsley
  3 tablespoons fresh lemon juice
Parsley sprigs (optional)

1. Preheat oven to 375°.
2. Combine eggplant, ⅛ teaspoon salt, 1
tablespoon oil, and black pepper in a bowl;
toss gently to coat. Arrange mixture in a
single layer on a baking sheet coated with
cooking spray. Bake at 375° for 45 minutes
or until eggplant is golden brown, turning
occasionally.
3. Place eggplant mixture in a large bowl;
mash with a potato masher. Stir in ⅛ teaspoon salt, ¾ cup water, paprika, cumin,
red pepper, and garlic.
4. Heat 1 tablespoon oil in a large nonstick skillet over medium-low heat. Add
eggplant mixture; cook 10 minutes or until
liquid almost evaporates, stirring occasionally. Stir in parsley and juice. Garnish

with parsley sprigs, if desired. Serve
with pita bread or fresh vegetables.
Yield: 12 servings (serving size: about 3
tablespoons).

CALORIES 44 (48% from fat); FAT 2.6g (sat 0.4g, mono 1.8g, poly 0.3g);
PROTEIN 0.9g; CARB 5.3g; FIBER 0.3g; CHOL 0mg; IRON 0.4mg;
SODIUM 248mg; CALC 11mg

entertaining tip

Create a special mood for your Moroccan
evening: Cover the table in colorful, rich
textiles, and serve the food in hand-
painted pottery. Have plenty of pita bread
on hand for guests to use to scoop up
food—it's a Moroccan tradition.

Citrus Chicken Tagine

A tagine is a Moroccan stew with chicken or some type of meat simmered with vegetables, olives, lemon, and garlic. It's usually flavored with such spices as ginger, pepper, and saffron, and served over couscous. Relax and enjoy a glass of wine while the stew simmers on the stove top.

Kuentz-Bas "Pfersigberg" Riesling

1½ teaspoons olive oil
  1 pound skinless, boneless chicken thighs, coarsely chopped
  1 cup chopped onion
 ½ cup chopped red bell pepper
 ¼ teaspoon ground ginger
 ¼ teaspoon ground cinnamon
 ⅛ teaspoon saffron threads, crushed
  2 garlic cloves, minced
 ½ cup fat-free, less-sodium chicken broth
 ½ cup orange juice
 ½ teaspoon salt
 ⅛ teaspoon black pepper
 ¾ cup chopped orange sections (about 1 orange)
  3 tablespoons chopped fresh parsley
  3 tablespoons chopped fresh cilantro
  2 tablespoons sliced pitted kalamata olives
  1 tablespoon chopped lemon sections (about ½ lemon)
2½ cups hot cooked couscous
    Flat-leaf parsley sprigs (optional)

1. Heat oil in a Dutch oven over medium heat. Add chicken and next 6 ingredients, and cook for 12 minutes. Stir in broth, juice, salt, and black pepper. Bring to a boil; cover, reduce heat, and simmer 30 minutes.
2. Remove chicken mixture from heat; stir in orange and next 4 ingredients. Serve over couscous; garnish with parsley, if desired. Yield: 4 servings (serving size: about 1 cup chicken mixture and ⅔ cup couscous).

CALORIES 331 (21% from fat); FAT 7.8g (sat 1.6g, mono 3.6g, poly 1.5g); PROTEIN 27.9g; CARB 36.5g; FIBER 3.8g; CHOL 94mg; IRON 2.2mg; SODIUM 459mg; CALC 58mg

Almond-Stuffed Dates

If you don't have a food grinder, you can use a food processor to grind the almonds, although the paste will not be as smooth.

Hidalgo Oloroso Especial Sherry

  1 cup whole blanched almonds
  1 tablespoon grated lemon rind
  2 tablespoons water
  6 tablespoons sugar
  1 tablespoon butter
24 large pitted dates
  3 tablespoons sugar

1. Preheat oven to 250°.
2. Place almonds on a baking sheet, and bake at 250° for 8 to 10 minutes or until warm. Slowly feed almonds through a food grinder fitted with a coarse plate. Switching to a fine grinding plate, feed almonds through grinder 3 or 4 times until smooth. Transfer to a bowl, and stir in lemon rind.
3. Combine 2 tablespoons water and 6 tablespoons sugar in a small saucepan; bring to a boil. Reduce heat to medium-high. Add butter and ground almonds, stirring vigorously until mixture leaves sides of pan. Transfer mixture to a small bowl. Cover and cool 5 minutes.
4. Cut a lengthwise slit down center of each date to (but not through) the bottom, leaving ends intact. Mold a heaping teaspoonful of almond paste into a football shape; stuff inside date. Gently press sides until paste pushes up slightly above top of date. Place 3 tablespoons sugar on a small plate. Roll each stuffed date lightly in sugar. Serve immediately. Yield: 2 dozen.
NOTE: One 7-ounce tube almond paste may be substituted for fresh almond mixture. Knead lemon rind into paste, and proceed with recipe.

CALORIES 124 (27% from fat); FAT 3.6g (sat 0.5g, mono 2.1g, poly 0.8g); PROTEIN 1.8g; CARB 23.9g; FIBER 2.3g; CHOL 1mg; IRON 0.4mg; SODIUM 5mg; CALC 29mg

about the wine

As Champagne is in France and Port is in Portugal, Sherry is the most complex, sophisticated, and labor-intensive wine produced in Spain. It is also quite possibly the world's most misunderstood wine, wrongly cast as a sugary nightcap. Sherry actually comes in seven styles, ranging from hauntingly bone dry to richly sweet. Oloroso, the perfect accompaniment with these stuffed dates, is as lush and sumptuous an experience as wine gets. (See pages 160 and 177 for more information on the styles of Sherry.) Besides being known for its wine, Sherry country is also one of Spain's most thrilling food regions, as well as the place where small dishes known as tapas were invented.

classic thanksgiving

For me, Thanksgiving is a profound reminder of the differences between dining and simply eating. Bright candles, cloth napkins, beautiful plates—and, all of a sudden, turkey and sweet potatoes are transformed into a celebration. The dishes that make up this menu are modest, but the experience is magical.

menu | wine

Apple Cider-Brined Turkey with Savory Herb Gravy

Mesclun and Romaine Salad with Vinaigrette

Herbed Bread Stuffing

Brown Sugar-Glazed Sweet Potato Wedges

Shredded Brussels Sprouts with Bacon and Hazelnuts

Cranberry Chutney

Dinner rolls

Pumpkin Pie with Pecan Pastry Crust

Pecan Pie with Cream

Serves 12

Because of wine's ineluctable ties to the harvest, it—more than any other beverage—genuinely manifests the idea of giving thanks. On Thanksgiving Day, if your home is like mine, the kitchen is command central, where everyone wants to linger. So as the seductive smells of the roasting turkey fill the room, I pour chilled flutes of California sparkling wine for everyone to enjoy while I'm putting the finishing touches on several dishes. I love many sparklers, but often for this dinner I'll pull out one of my favorites: **Roederer Estate Anderson Valley Brut** ($$).

Traditionally, for Thanksgiving, the savory dishes are served all at once, other than in multiple courses, so I offer a single majestic red. Being able to complement everything from an herb-mushroom-sausage stuffing to brown sugar-caramelized sweet potatoes to cranberry chutney and the delicious bird itself is a tall order for any red. But one wine truly excels: Châteauneuf-du-Pape, from the southern Rhône Valley of France. Made primarily from grenache, syrah, and mourvèdre grapes, **Domaine Font De Michelle Châteauneuf-du-Pape** ($$$$) is stupendous, suffused with dark chocolate, grenadine, espresso, and cherry jam flavors. It's got the grip to stand up to every dish here, with an elegance that makes it seductive.

Thanksgiving needs to have a celebratory finale. So what goes magnificently with pumpkin and pecan pies? Tawny Port. The roasted nuts and rich toffee character of **Taylor Fladgate 20 Year Old Tawny Porto** ($$$$) highlights the rich sweetness of the pumpkin and the profound nuttiness of the pecan pie in a way that has to be tasted to be believed.

Roederer Estate Anderson Valley Brut

Domaine Font De Michelle Châteauneuf-du-Pape

Taylor Fladgate 20 Year Old Tawny Porto

Apple Cider-Brined Turkey with Savory Herb Gravy

Brining is an overnight process, so be sure to allow yourself enough time. Use two turkey-sized plastic oven bags to prevent the brine from leaking, and place the turkey in a large stockpot as another precaution. The spiced apple cider brine adds just the right amount of tangy sweetness to the bird.

Domaine Font De Michelle Châteauneuf-du-Pape

BRINE:

- 8 cups apple cider
- ⅔ cup kosher salt
- ⅔ cup sugar
- 1 tablespoon black peppercorns, coarsely crushed
- 1 tablespoon whole allspice, coarsely crushed
- 8 (⅛-inch-thick) slices peeled fresh ginger
- 6 whole cloves
- 2 bay leaves
- 1 (12-pound) fresh turkey
- 2 oranges, quartered
- 6 cups ice

REMAINING INGREDIENTS:

- 4 garlic cloves
- 4 sage leaves
- 4 thyme sprigs
- 4 parsley sprigs
- 1 onion, quartered
- 1 (14-ounce) can fat-free, less-sodium chicken broth
- 2 tablespoons unsalted butter, melted and divided
- 1 teaspoon freshly ground black pepper, divided
- ½ teaspoon salt, divided
- Savory Herb Gravy (see recipe at right)
- Fresh herbs (optional)
- Orange wedges (optional)

1. To prepare brine, combine first 8 ingredients in a large saucepan; bring to a boil. Cook 5 minutes or until salt and sugar dissolve. Cool completely.

2. Remove giblets and neck from turkey; reserve for Savory Herb Gravy. Rinse turkey with cold water; pat dry. Trim excess fat. Stuff body cavity of turkey with orange quarters. Place a turkey-sized oven bag inside a second bag to form a double thickness. Place bags in a large stockpot. Place turkey inside inner bag. Add cider mixture and ice. Secure bags with several twist ties. Refrigerate 12 to 24 hours, turning occasionally.

3. Preheat oven to 500°.

4. Remove turkey from bags, and discard brine, orange quarters, and bags. Rinse turkey with cold water; pat dry. Lift wing tips up and over back; tuck under turkey. Tie legs together with kitchen string. Place garlic, sage, thyme, parsley, onion, and broth in bottom of a roasting pan. Place roasting rack in pan. Arrange turkey, breast side down, on roasting rack. Brush turkey back with 1 tablespoon butter; sprinkle with ½ teaspoon pepper and ¼ teaspoon salt. Bake at 500° for 30 minutes.

5. Reduce oven temperature to 350°.

6. Remove turkey from oven. Carefully turn turkey over (breast side up) using tongs. Brush turkey breast with 1 tablespoon butter; sprinkle with ½ teaspoon pepper and ¼ teaspoon salt. Bake at 350° for 1 hour and 15 minutes or until a thermometer inserted into meaty part of thigh registers 170° (make sure not to touch bone). (Shield turkey with foil if it browns too quickly.) Remove turkey from oven; let stand 20 minutes. Reserve pan drippings for Savory Herb Gravy. Discard skin before serving; serve with gravy. If desired, garnish with fresh herbs and orange wedges. Yield: 12 servings (serving size: 6 ounces turkey and about 3 tablespoons gravy).

(Totals include Savory Herb Gravy) CALORIES 338 (30% from fat); FAT 11.3g (sat 4.2g, mono 2.5g, poly 3.0g); PROTEIN 51.3g; CARB 4.5g; FIBER 0.1g; CHOL 138mg; IRON 3.3mg; SODIUM 770mg; CALC 45mg

SAVORY HERB GRAVY

- 2 teaspoons vegetable oil
- Reserved turkey giblets and neck
- 4 cups water
- 6 black peppercorns
- 4 parsley sprigs
- 2 thyme sprigs
- 1 yellow onion, unpeeled and quartered
- 1 carrot, cut into 2-inch pieces
- 1 celery stalk, cut into 2-inch pieces
- 1 bay leaf
- Reserved turkey drippings
- 3 tablespoons all-purpose flour
- ½ teaspoon salt
- ¼ teaspoon freshly ground black pepper

1. Heat oil in a large saucepan over medium-high heat. Add turkey giblets and neck; cook 5 minutes, browning on all sides. Add water and next 7 ingredients; bring to a boil. Reduce heat, and simmer until liquid is reduced to about 2½ cups (about 1 hour). Strain cooking liquid through a colander into a bowl, reserving cooking liquid and turkey neck. Discard remaining solids. Chill cooking liquid completely. Skim fat from surface, and discard. Remove meat from neck; finely chop meat. Discard neck bone. Add neck meat to cooking liquid.

2. Strain reserved turkey drippings through a colander into a shallow bowl; discard solids. Place strained drippings in freezer 20 minutes. Skim fat from surface; discard.

3. Place flour in a medium saucepan; add ¼ cup cooking liquid, stirring with a whisk until smooth. Add remaining cooking liquid, turkey drippings, salt, and pepper; bring to a boil, stirring frequently. Reduce heat; simmer 5 minutes or until slightly thickened. Yield: 2½ cups (serving size: about 3 tablespoons).

CALORIES 21 (43% from fat); FAT 1.0g (sat 0.2g, mono 0.2g, poly 0.5g); PROTEIN 1.3g; CARB 1.7g; FIBER 0.1g; CHOL 4mg; IRON 0.2mg; SODIUM 160mg; CALC 2mg

entertaining tip

Now is the time to bring out your china and use all of the platters, plates, and serving dishes. Don't be afraid to mix and match, especially if you have a collection of vintage serving dishes. Use salt dishes and salt spoons for kosher salt and freshly ground pepper; these seasonings make a big difference in flavor.

Mesclun and Romaine Salad with Vinaigrette

Dress up a typical salad by using gourmet greens, adding fresh herbs, and tossing with high-quality olive oil and Sherry vinegar.

Domaine Font De Michelle Châteauneuf-du-Pape

VINAIGRETTE:
- 3 tablespoons minced shallots
- 1½ tablespoons Sherry vinegar
- 1 tablespoon extravirgin olive oil
- ½ teaspoon salt
- ½ teaspoon Dijon mustard
- ¼ teaspoon freshly ground black pepper

SALAD:
- 4 cups mesclun (gourmet salad greens)
- 4 cups torn romaine lettuce
- 2 cups diced pear
- ¼ cup chopped fresh basil
- ¼ cup chopped fresh parsley

1. To prepare vinaigrette, combine shallots and vinegar in a small bowl; let stand 5 minutes. Add oil, salt, mustard, and pepper; stir well with a whisk.

2. To prepare salad, place salad greens and remaining 4 ingredients in a large bowl; toss gently to combine. Drizzle vinaigrette over salad, and toss gently to coat. Yield: 12 servings (serving size: 1 cup).

CALORIES 36 (38% from fat); FAT 1.5g (sat 0.2g, mono 0.8g, poly 0.2g); PROTEIN 0.8g; CARB 5.9g; FIBER 1.6g; CHOL 0mg; IRON 0.6mg; SODIUM 108mg; CALC 34mg

Herbed Bread Stuffing

Mushrooms and sausage add hearty flavor to this rustic-style stuffing.

Domaine Font De Michelle Châteauneuf-du-Pape

- 1½ pounds peasant-style white bread
- 4 (4-ounce) links sweet turkey Italian sausage
- 2 teaspoons butter
- 1 pound cremini mushrooms, quartered
- Cooking spray
- 2 cups chopped onion
- 1¼ cups chopped carrot
- 1¼ cups chopped celery
- ½ cup minced fresh parsley
- 1 tablespoon fresh thyme leaves
- 1 tablespoon minced fresh sage
- ½ teaspoon salt
- ¼ teaspoon freshly ground black pepper
- 2 large eggs, lightly beaten
- 1 (14-ounce) can fat-free, less-sodium chicken broth

1. Preheat oven to 400°.

2. Trim crust from bread. Cut bread into cubes; arrange cubes in a single layer on 2 jelly-roll pans. Bake at 400° for 10 minutes.

3. Reduce oven temperature to 350°.

4. Cook sausage in a skillet over medium-high heat 10 minutes, browning on all sides. Remove from pan and slice.

5. Melt butter in pan over medium-high heat. Add mushrooms; sauté 4 minutes. Combine bread, sausage, and mushrooms.

6. Heat pan over medium-high heat; coat with cooking spray. Add onion, carrot, and celery; sauté 5 minutes. Add parsley, thyme, sage, salt, and pepper; sauté 1 minute. Add to bread mixture. Combine eggs and broth, stirring with a whisk. Add to bread mixture; toss. Spoon into a 13 x 9-inch baking dish coated with cooking spray. Bake at 350° for 45 minutes. Yield: 12 servings (serving size: about 1 cup).

CALORIES 208 (27% from fat); FAT 6.2g (sat 1.7g, mono 1.9g, poly 1.2g); PROTEIN 13.6g; CARB 25.9g; FIBER 4.1g; CHOL 68mg; IRON 2mg; SODIUM 635mg; CALC 46mg

Herbed Bread Stuffing

Brown Sugar-Glazed Sweet Potato Wedges

The flavors of sweet potato casserole are featured here in tender wedges.

Domaine Font De Michelle Châteauneuf-du-Pape

¼ cup unsalted butter
¾ cup packed dark brown sugar
¼ cup water
1 teaspoon salt
½ teaspoon ground nutmeg
¼ teaspoon ground ginger
1 (3-inch) cinnamon stick
4 pounds sweet potatoes, peeled, cut in half crosswise, and cut into ½-inch wedges
Cooking spray

1. Preheat oven to 400°.
2. Melt butter in a medium saucepan over medium heat. Add sugar and next 5 ingredients; bring to a simmer. Cook 5 minutes, stirring frequently. Discard cinnamon stick. Combine sugar mixture and potato wedges in a large bowl; toss well to coat. Arrange potato mixture on a large jelly-roll pan coated with cooking spray. Bake at 400° for 40 minutes or until tender, stirring after 20 minutes. Yield: 12 servings (serving size: ⅔ cup).

CALORIES 182 (19% from fat); FAT 3.9g (sat 2.4g, mono 1.1g, poly 0.2g); PROTEIN 1.7g; CARB 36.1g; FIBER 3.0g; CHOL 10mg; IRON 0.8mg; SODIUM 211mg; CALC 44mg

Shredded Brussels Sprouts with Bacon and Hazelnuts

Sautéing Brussels sprouts in a skillet with bacon drippings may be the tastiest and quickest way to cook them. Slice the Brussels sprouts very thinly with a knife, or use the thin slicing blade attachment of a food processor.

Domaine Font De Michelle Châteauneuf-du-Pape

½ cup chopped bacon (about 3 slices)
½ cup fat-free, less-sodium chicken broth
13 cups thinly sliced Brussels sprouts (about 2 pounds)
1 teaspoon salt
½ teaspoon freshly ground black pepper
3 tablespoons chopped hazelnuts, toasted

1. Cook bacon in a large Dutch oven over medium-high heat 4 minutes or until crisp. Remove bacon from pan, reserving 1½ teaspoons drippings in pan. Add broth to pan; bring to a simmer. Add Brussels sprouts; cook 4 minutes or until crisp-tender, stirring frequently. Sprinkle with salt and pepper, tossing gently to combine. Sprinkle evenly with bacon and hazelnuts. Serve immediately. Yield: 12 servings (serving size: ¾ cup).

CALORIES 59 (41% from fat); FAT 2.7g (sat 0.7g, mono 1.5g, poly 0.4g); PROTEIN 3.4g; CARB 7.2g; FIBER 3.1g; CHOL 2mg; IRON 1.2mg; SODIUM 262mg; CALC 35mg

Cranberry Chutney

Slivered almonds add crunch to this fresh berry chutney.

Domaine Font De Michelle Châteauneuf-du-Pape

4 cups fresh cranberries
2 cups packed brown sugar
1 cup raisins
1 cup water
½ cup slivered almonds, toasted
¼ cup fresh lemon juice
1 teaspoon salt
1 teaspoon grated onion
⅛ teaspoon ground cloves

1. Combine all ingredients in a large saucepan, and bring to a boil. Reduce heat, and simmer 35 minutes or until thickened. Yield: 3½ cups (serving size: ¼ cup).

CALORIES 199 (11% from fat); FAT 2.5g (sat 0.2g, mono 1.6g, poly 0.6g); PROTEIN 1.4g; CARB 44.2g; FIBER 2.2g; CHOL 0mg; IRON 1.2mg; SODIUM 184mg; CALC 47mg

Wine is the only natural beverage that feeds not only the body, but the soul and spirit of man.

—Robert Mondavi, winemaker

entertaining tip

If your set table is too full for a centerpiece, add color to the dining room by placing fresh produce (such as squash and pumpkins) and autumn leaves on the windowsill.

Apple Cider-Brined Turkey with Savory Herb Gravy, Shredded Brussels Sprouts with Bacon and Hazelnuts, Brown Sugar-Glazed Sweet Potato Wedges, Cranberry Chutney, Herbed Bread Stuffing

Pecan Pie with Cream,
Pumpkin Pie with Pecan Pastry Crust

Pumpkin Pie with Pecan Pastry Crust

To make sure you get the best pecan flavor in the crust, use fresh pecans and grind them in a food processor or spice grinder.

Taylor Fladgate 20 Year Old Tawny Porto

CRUST:

1   cup all-purpose flour, divided
3½   tablespoons ice water
1   teaspoon fresh lemon juice
3   tablespoons ground pecans, toasted
2   tablespoons powdered sugar
¼   teaspoon salt
3   tablespoons vegetable shortening
Cooking spray

FILLING:

1   cup fat-free sour cream
⅓   cup granulated sugar
2   tablespoons molasses
1½   teaspoons pumpkin-pie spice
1   teaspoon vanilla extract
¼   teaspoon salt
2   large egg whites, lightly beaten
1   large egg, lightly beaten
1   (15-ounce) can pumpkin

1. Preheat oven to 350°.

2. To prepare crust, lightly spoon flour into a dry measuring cup, and level with a knife. Combine ¼ cup flour, ice water, and lemon juice, stirring with a whisk until well blended to form a slurry. Combine ¾ cup flour, pecans, powdered sugar, and ¼ teaspoon salt in a large bowl; cut in shortening with a pastry blender or 2 knives until mixture resembles coarse meal. Add slurry; toss with a fork until flour mixture is moist.

3. Gently press mixture into a 4-inch circle on 2 sheets of overlapping heavy-duty plastic wrap; cover with 2 additional sheets of overlapping plastic wrap. Roll dough, still covered, into a 12-inch circle. Freeze dough 10 minutes or until plastic wrap can be easily removed.

4. Remove dough from freezer. Remove top 2 sheets of plastic wrap; let dough stand 1 minute or until pliable. Fit dough, plastic wrap side up, into a 9-inch pie plate coated with cooking spray, allowing dough to extend over edge. Remove remaining plastic wrap. Press dough into bottom and up sides of pie plate. Fold edges under, and flute. Place in freezer until ready to fill.

5. To prepare filling, combine sour cream and remaining 8 ingredients, stirring with a whisk until well blended. Pour filling into prepared crust. Bake at 350° for 45 minutes or until a knife inserted in center comes out clean; cool on a wire rack. Yield: 8 servings (serving size: 1 wedge).

CALORIES 234 (30% from fat); FAT 7.9g (sat 1.9g, mono 2.9g, poly 1.9g); PROTEIN 5.6g; CARB 35.8g; FIBER 2.5g; CHOL 29mg; IRON 2.1mg; SODIUM 322mg; CALC 83mg

Pecan Pie with Cream

Brown rice syrup is a sweetener with soft, delicate flavor. It's sold in the baking section of supermarkets and health-food stores.

Taylor Fladgate 20 Year Old Tawny Porto

CRUST:

1   cup all-purpose flour
3   tablespoons ice water
1   teaspoon fresh lemon juice
2   tablespoons powdered sugar
¼   teaspoon salt
3   tablespoons vegetable shortening
Cooking spray

FILLING:

1   cup brown rice syrup or dark corn syrup
¼   cup maple syrup
2   tablespoons all-purpose flour
¼   teaspoon salt
2   large eggs
1   large egg white
½   cup pecan halves
1   teaspoon vanilla extract

TOPPING:

⅔   cup whipped cream

1. Preheat oven to 350°.

2. To prepare crust, lightly spoon 1 cup flour into a dry measuring cup, and level with a knife. Combine ¼ cup flour, ice water, and lemon juice, stirring with a whisk until well blended to form a slurry. Combine ¾ cup flour, powdered sugar, and ¼ teaspoon salt in a large bowl; cut in shortening with a pastry blender or 2 knives until mixture resembles coarse meal. Add slurry; toss with a fork until flour mixture is moist.

3. Gently press mixture into a 4-inch circle on 2 sheets of overlapping heavy-duty plastic wrap; cover with 2 additional sheets of overlapping plastic wrap. Roll dough, still covered, into a 12-inch circle. Freeze dough 10 minutes or until plastic wrap can be easily removed.

4. Remove dough from freezer. Remove top 2 sheets of plastic wrap; let dough stand 1 minute or until pliable. Fit dough, plastic wrap side up, into a 9-inch pie plate coated with cooking spray, allowing dough to extend over edge. Remove remaining plastic wrap. Press dough into bottom and up sides of pie plate. Fold edges under; flute. Bake at 350° for 8 minutes. Cool on wire rack.

5. To prepare filling, place rice syrup and next 5 ingredients in a large bowl; beat with a mixer at medium speed until well blended. Stir in pecans and vanilla. Pour filling into prepared crust. Bake at 350° for 50 minutes or until edges puff and center is set (shield edges of piecrust with foil if crust gets too brown). Cool on wire rack. Top each serving with whipped cream. Yield: 10 servings (serving size: 1 wedge and about 1 tablespoon whipped cream).

CALORIES 268 (29% from fat); FAT 8.6g (sat 1.6g, mono 3.9g, poly 2.3g); PROTEIN 3.6g; CARB 45.3g; FIBER 0.7g; CHOL 42mg; IRON 1.2mg; SODIUM 190mg; CALC 19mg

winter

If food is the body of good living, wine is its soul.

—Clifton Fadiman, American author

There's a moment in late fall (I think of it as "the apple pie moment") when the cold air suddenly turns sharp and the light is so clear and piercing that it seems like crystal. In that moment, I'm struck by the desire to bake an apple pie—and I know then that winter has arrived. *Finally!* I think to myself, for I'm secretly thrilled. Winter, after all, is the perfect excuse to stay inside and cook. Whereas most seasons beckon you outside—to the garden, to the beach, to the park—winter draws you indoors into the sanctuary of your own kitchen. Maybe it's because I like spending so much time in the

> To me, the wines that feel right in winter have a high soul-satisfying quotient.

kitchen during winter that I also love slow-cooked foods that simmer for hours, filling the house with impossibly irresistible smells. Soups, ragoûts, stews, and roasts—comfort foods by nature—are quintessential wintertime fare. They're comfortable to make and to eat and, most of all, comfortable to enjoy in the company of a bottle of good wine. To me, the wines (and foods) that just feel right in winter have a high soul-satisfying quotient. Often rich and generous, wintertime wines are meant to be savored slowly, for they inspire awe—like winter itself.

holiday dinner

Most of the year I like to entertain simply, but the holidays inspire me to pull out all the stops. The smell of starched linens, the heft of good silver, and the feel of my best wine glasses add to a menu of luscious dishes and truly great wines for what I call "sense memories," worthy of treasuring forever.

menu | wine

Golden Oyster Bisque

Beef Tenderloin with Parsnip-Mushroom Ragoût

Wild Rice and Walnut Pilaf

Steamed Green Beans

Buttermilk-Chive Biscuits

Double-Coconut Cake with Fluffy Coconut Frosting

Serves 12

For me, a classic holiday dinner party must begin with glasses of chilled Champagne, and so I select the first course accordingly. Often, that choice is creamy Golden Oyster Bisque. The Champagne's creaminess mirrors that of the bisque, and the minerality of the bone-dry Champagne underscores the briny oyster flavor. The textures are a fascinating contrast: The bubbles are lively and brisk; the bisque is thick and creamy. A stellar match is **Veuve Clicquot Ponsardin Brut Champagne** ($$$$).

Veuve Clicquot Ponsardin Brut Champagne

Just thinking about the rich flavor of roasted beef tenderloin makes me crave a well-structured, highly concentrated merlot. Definitely dinner-party material, **Chappellet Merlot** ($$$), from California's Napa Valley, has the stature to stand up to such a sophisticated beef dish as this. The wine's ripe red plumminess framed by a delicious burst of vanilla is a perfect complement to the sweet earthiness of the parsnip- and mushroom-accented ragoût.

Chappellet Merlot

Schramsberg Crémant Demi-Sec

Double-Coconut Cake is a showstopper of a dessert, especially when it's served with a tall glass of **Schramsberg Crémant Demi-Sec** ($$$), a lightly sweet sparkling dessert wine from California. The rush of tingling bubbles juxtaposed with the creamy, light frosting creates an unbelievably captivating texture on your palate. And this crémant demi-sec has just the right whisper of sweetness to counterbalance the full-throttle scrumptiousness of the coconut. After tasting dozens of combinations of dessert wines and desserts, I have to say that this is one of the most majestically delicious matches of all time. To begin and end a dinner party with bubbles brings a celebration full circle. It's a special touch I do only during the holidays—and looking at my guests, I know there's something purely magical about it.

Beef Tenderloin with
Parsnip-Mushroom Ragoût

Golden Oyster Bisque

Saffron colors this holiday favorite a rich yellow-gold.

Veuve Clicquot Ponsardin Brut Champagne

2 (8-ounce) containers standard oysters, undrained
1 (8-ounce) bottle clam juice
1 tablespoon hot water
¼ teaspoon saffron threads, crushed
1 teaspoon butter
1 cup coarsely chopped red onion
1 cup coarsely chopped celery
¼ cup all-purpose flour
¼ teaspoon ground coriander seeds
3 cups 2% reduced-fat milk
¼ cup chopped fresh flat-leaf parsley
¼ teaspoon salt
⅛ teaspoon ground red pepper

1. Drain oysters in a colander over a bowl, reserving liquid. Add enough clam juice to oyster liquid to equal 1 cup, and set aside. Reserve remaining clam juice for another use. Coarsely chop oysters.
2. Combine water and saffron in a small bowl; set aside.
3. Melt butter in a large saucepan over medium heat. Add chopped onion and celery, and cook for 5 minutes, stirring frequently. Lightly spoon flour into a dry measuring cup, and level with a knife. Stir flour and coriander into onion mixture, and cook 1 minute. Add oyster liquid mixture, saffron water, and milk, stirring with a whisk. Cook until thick (about 12 minutes), stirring frequently. Add oysters, parsley, salt, and pepper. Cook 3 minutes or until edges of oysters curl. Yield 12 servings (serving size ½ cup).

CALORIES 77 (30% from fat); FAT 2.6g (sat 1.6g, mono 0.6g, poly 0.4g); PROTEIN 5.3g; CARB 8.1g; FIBER 0.6g; CHOL 27mg; IRON 2.9mg; SODIUM 157mg; CALC 103mg

Beef Tenderloin with Parsnip-Mushroom Ragoût

The sweet parsnips and woodsy porcini mushrooms create a flavorful sauce for beef tenderloin.

Chappellet Merlot

RAGOÛT:
1½ cups boiling water
2 cups dried porcini mushrooms (about 2 ounces)
2 teaspoons butter
½ cup chopped shallots
3 tablespoons minced garlic
1 teaspoon minced fresh or ¼ teaspoon dried thyme
3 cups coarsely chopped parsnips (about 1 pound)
12 cups quartered button mushrooms (about 1½ pounds)
½ cup Port wine
2 tablespoons chopped fresh parsley
½ teaspoon salt
½ teaspoon freshly ground black pepper

BEEF:
½ teaspoon salt
½ teaspoon freshly ground black pepper
1 (3-pound) beef tenderloin, trimmed and cut in half crosswise
Cooking spray

SAUCE:
1 teaspoon butter
⅓ cup (2-inch) julienne-cut carrot
⅓ cup vertically sliced shallots
¼ cup Port wine
1 (14-ounce) can less-sodium beef broth
¼ teaspoon salt
¼ teaspoon freshly ground black pepper

1. To prepare ragoût, pour boiling water over porcini; let stand 20 minutes. Strain through a sieve into a bowl; reserve liquid. Finely chop porcini; divide in half.
2. Melt 2 teaspoons butter in a large nonstick skillet over medium heat. Add ½ cup shallots, garlic, and thyme; cook 1 minute, stirring frequently. Add parsnips; cook 2 minutes, stirring occasionally. Add button mushrooms; cook 10 minutes, stirring occasionally. Add half of porcini and ½ cup wine; bring to a boil. Cover, reduce heat, and cook 15 minutes or until parsnips are tender. Stir in parsley, ½ teaspoon salt, and ½ teaspoon pepper. Set aside; keep warm.
3. Preheat oven to 450°.
4. To prepare beef, rub ½ teaspoon salt and ½ teaspoon pepper over tenderloin. Heat a large ovenproof skillet over medium-high heat. Coat pan with cooking spray. Add tenderloin; cook 5 minutes, browning on all sides. Bake at 450° for 20 minutes or until a thermometer registers 140° (medium-rare) or desired degree of doneness. Place tenderloin on a cutting board; cover loosely with foil. Let stand 10 minutes. (Temperature of tenderloin will increase 5° upon standing.)
5. To prepare sauce, melt 1 teaspoon butter in pan over medium-high heat. Add carrot and ⅓ cup shallots; sauté 3 minutes. Add reserved porcini liquid, remaining porcini, ¼ cup wine, and broth; bring to a boil. Cook until reduced to 1½ cups (about 10 minutes). Stir in ¼ teaspoon salt and ¼ teaspoon pepper. Cut beef into thin slices; serve with ragoût and sauce. Yield: 12 servings (serving size: 3 ounces tenderloin, ⅔ cup ragoût, and 2 tablespoons sauce).

CALORIES 265 (35% from fat); FAT 10.3g (sat 3.9g, mono 3.8g, poly 0.6g); PROTEIN 28.8g; CARB 14.1g; FIBER 3.4g; CHOL 74mg; IRON 5.2mg; SODIUM 330mg; CALC 36mg

wine tip

Brown and wild rice have a deep, earthy graininess that is beautifully complemented by a wine with noticeable oak flavors. The same is true for toasted nuts, their nuttiness acting as a bridge to the wine's oaky flavors. While many wines in the world are made in a style that emphasizes oak, big California reds—such as merlot, cabernet sauvignon, syrah, and zinfandel—are virtually always dependable on this score.

Wild Rice and Walnut Pilaf

A hearty rice pilaf, flavored with a touch of mild herbs, is a perfect partner for beef tenderloin.

Chappellet Merlot

    1   tablespoon butter
    ¾   cup finely chopped onion
    4½ cups water
    2¼ cups long-grain brown and wild rice
        blend (such as Lundberg's)
    1½ teaspoons salt, divided
    ⅓   cup chopped fresh parsley
    3   tablespoons chopped fresh chives
    3   tablespoons fresh lemon juice
    1   tablespoon olive oil
    ⅓   cup chopped walnuts, toasted

1. Melt butter in a small saucepan over medium heat. Add onion; cook 3 minutes, stirring frequently. Stir in water, rice, and ¾ teaspoon salt; bring to a boil. Cover, reduce heat, and simmer 40 minutes or until liquid is absorbed. Remove from heat; stir in ¾ teaspoon salt, parsley, chives, juice, and oil. Sprinkle with walnuts. Yield: 12 servings (serving size: ⅔ cup).

CALORIES 177 (28% from fat); FAT 5.5g (sat 1.2g, mono 1.8g, poly 2.3g); PROTEIN 3.5g; CARB 29.0g; FIBER 1.7g; CHOL 3mg; IRON 0.9mg; SODIUM 308mg; CALC 24mg

Steamed Green Beans

There's no need to make things complicated when you're preparing a lot of dishes for a big meal. A splash of walnut oil and a bit of salt and pepper are all you need on this simple steamed vegetable.

Chappellet Merlot

    2   pounds green beans, trimmed
    1   tablespoon walnut oil
    ½   teaspoon salt
    ¼   teaspoon freshly ground black pepper

1. Steam green beans, covered, 5 minutes or until crisp-tender. Drain and return to pan. Add oil, salt, and pepper; toss to coat. Serve immediately. Yield: 12 servings (serving size: ⅔ cup).

CALORIES 33 (30% from fat); FAT 1.1g (sat 0.1g, mono 0.3g, poly 0.7g); PROTEIN 0.9g; CARB 4.7g; FIBER 2.8g; CHOL 0mg; IRON 0.4mg; SODIUM 98mg; CALC 38mg

wine tip

A top-notch merlot and a top-notch cabernet sauvignon are very similar in form, weight, flavor, and cost. Each has a lot of tannin, a compound in grape skins and seeds that gives the resulting wine a sense of imposing structure. And both have aromas and flavors evocative of red fruits, cassis, cocoa, vanilla, and tobacco. As a result, merlot and cabernet sauvignon are often interchangeable when it comes to food-and-wine pairings. If one goes well with a dish, chances are that the other will, too.

Buttermilk-Chive Biscuits

Fresh chives add a mild onion flavor to these tender little biscuits.

Chappellet Merlot

    2   cups all-purpose flour
    1   tablespoon baking powder
    ½   teaspoon baking soda
    ½   teaspoon salt
    ¼   cup chilled butter, cut into small pieces
    ¾   cup low-fat buttermilk
    1   large egg, lightly beaten
    ¼   cup chopped fresh chives

1. Preheat oven to 400°.
2. Lightly spoon flour into dry measuring cups; level with a knife. Combine flour, baking powder, baking soda, and salt in a large bowl; cut in butter with a pastry blender or 2 knives until mixture resembles coarse meal. Combine buttermilk and egg, and stir in chives. Add buttermilk mixture to flour mixture, and stir just until moist.
3. Turn dough out onto a heavily floured surface; knead lightly 5 times. Roll dough to a ½-inch thickness; cut with a 2-inch biscuit cutter. Place dough rounds, 1 inch apart, on a baking sheet. Bake at 400° for 12 minutes or until golden. Serve warm or at room temperature. Yield: 20 biscuits (serving size: 1 biscuit).

CALORIES 74 (33% from fat); FAT 2.7g (sat 1.6g, mono 0.8g, poly 0.2g); PROTEIN 2.0g; CARB 10.2g; FIBER 0.4g; CHOL 17mg; IRON 0.7mg; SODIUM 199mg; CALC 56mg

Steamed Green Beans,
Wild Rice and Walnut Pilaf, Beef
Tenderloin with Parsnip-Mushroom Ragoût

entertaining tip

Holiday table decorations don't have to be ornate to be impressive. It's elegant to keep it simple with a few candles and sprigs of rosemary placed on a white platter.

Double-Coconut Cake with Fluffy Coconut Frosting

The rich sweetness of coconut abounds in this tender cake because of the addition of coconut milk to the batter. Also, the fluffy frosting is flavored with coconut extract and topped with flaked coconut, resulting in a decadent holiday dessert.

Schramsberg Crémant Demi-Sec

Cooking spray
1   tablespoon sifted cake flour
2¼   cups sifted cake flour
2¼   teaspoons baking powder
½   teaspoon salt
1⅔   cups sugar
⅓   cup butter, softened
2   large eggs
1   (14-ounce) can light coconut milk
1   tablespoon vanilla extract
Fluffy Coconut Frosting
⅔   cup flaked sweetened coconut, divided

1. Preheat oven to 350°.
2. Coat 2 (9-inch) round cake pans with cooking spray; dust with 1 tablespoon flour.
3. Combine 2¼ cups flour, baking powder, and salt, stirring with a whisk. Place sugar and butter in a large bowl, and beat with a mixer at medium speed until well blended (about 5 minutes). Add eggs, 1 at a time, beating well after each addition. Add flour mixture and coconut milk alternately to sugar mixture, beginning and ending with flour mixture. Stir in vanilla.
4. Pour batter into prepared pans. Sharply tap pans once on counter to remove air bubbles. Bake at 350° for 30 minutes or until a wooden pick inserted in center comes out clean. Cool 10 minutes on wire racks; remove from pans. Cool completely on wire racks.
5. Place 1 cake layer on a plate; spread with 1 cup Fluffy Coconut Frosting. Sprinkle with ⅓ cup coconut. Top with remaining cake layer; spread remaining frosting over top and sides of cake. Sprinkle ⅓ cup coconut over top of cake. Yield: 14 servings (serving size: 1 slice).

(Totals include Fluffy Coconut Frosting) CALORIES 298 (24% from fat); FAT 7.9g (sat 5.0g, mono 1.7g, poly 0.3g); PROTEIN 3.4g; CARB 53.8g; FIBER 0.4g; CHOL 42mg; IRON 1.6mg; SODIUM 273mg; CALC 52mg

FLUFFY COCONUT FROSTING
4   large egg whites
½   teaspoon cream of tartar
Dash of salt
1   cup sugar
¼   cup water
½   teaspoon vanilla extract
¼   teaspoon coconut extract

1. Place egg whites, cream of tartar, and salt in a large bowl; beat with a mixer at high speed until stiff peaks form. Combine sugar and water in a saucepan; bring to a boil. Cook, without stirring, until a candy thermometer registers 238°. Pour hot sugar syrup in a thin stream over egg whites, beating at high speed. Stir in extracts. Yield: about 4 cups (serving size: about ¼ cup).

CALORIES 54 (0% from fat); FAT 0g (sat 0.0g, mono 0.0g, poly 0.0g); PROTEIN 0.9g; CARB 12.7g; FIBER 0g; CHOL 0mg; IRON 0mg; SODIUM 32mg; CALC 1mg

about the wine

Historically, Champagnes labeled *crémant* (French for "creamy") had a bit less effervescence and so tasted a touch softer than regular Champagnes. The term *demi-sec* translates from French to English as "half dry," or slightly sweet. Schramsberg Crémant Demi-Sec, a sparkling wine from California, is made from a rare grape variety called flora, which is a cross of semillon and gewürztraminer.

Chocolate Cheesecake

holiday dessert party

Here's the perfect holiday indulgence: four world-famous wines and the simple, exquisite desserts that accompany them best. With these matches, profoundly intense and pure flavors explode like fireworks on the palate.

menu | wine

Gingerbread

Chocolate Cheesecake

Poached Pears with Raspberry Sauce

Classic Sugar Cookies

Serves 8 to 12

Madeira's stunning toffee, honey, caramel, and brown sugar character is a knockout with the earthy, spicy, and molasses flavors of gingerbread. **Cossart Gordon 10 Year Old Bual Madeira** ($$$$), from Portugal, is as luscious and hauntingly complex as the gingerbread itself.

Rich, powerful, and oozingly soft, Port is considered the most "masculine" of the famous sweet wines. Deeply berried and chocolaty, it's also one of the few wines that work flawlessly with chocolate. Of the numerous styles, a plush vintage Port, such as **W. & J. Graham's Vintage Port** ($$$$$), from Portugal, is best—especially given the density and creaminess of this chocolate cheesecake.

Pure and vivid, Poached Pears with Raspberry Sauce has exactly the flavors needed to mirror the riveting bolt of peaches, apricots, and pears in a German riesling at the *beerenauslese* (BA) level of ripeness (see page 97). Sheer and ethereal, German BA has an elegance that is unreal—and unmatched. BAs are always made in tiny quantities so virtually any you find should be stunning. I adore **Müller-Catoir Haardter Bürgergarten Rieslaner Beerenauslese** ($$$$$ for a 375-milliliter half bottle), from the Mosel-Saar-Ruwer region of Germany.

Finally, serve Sauternes, the heralded dessert wine of Bordeaux. With its dizzyingly rich apricot flavors, Sauternes detonates on the palate and then spreads over your taste buds like melted honey. Utterly simple desserts, such as Classic Sugar Cookies, are the ultimate match. **Château d'Yquem Sauternes** ($$$$$) is a tour de force that's wildly expensive—and worth every nectarlike drop.

*Cossart Gordon
10 Year Old Bual Madeira*

W. & J. Graham's Vintage Port

*Müller-Catoir Haardter
Bürgergarten Rieslaner
Beerenauslese*

Château d'Yquem Sauternes

Gingerbread

Old-fashioned gingerbread has always been one of my favorites. It's not too sweet but has just the right touch of spiciness from ginger, nutmeg, and cloves.

Cossart Gordon 10 Year Old Bual Madeira

- ⅓ cup granulated sugar
- ¼ cup butter, softened
- ⅓ cup molasses
- 1 large egg
- 1½ cups all-purpose flour
- 1 teaspoon ground ginger
- ½ teaspoon baking soda
- ¼ teaspoon ground nutmeg
- ⅛ teaspoon salt
- ⅛ teaspoon ground cloves
- ⅔ cup 1% low-fat milk

Cooking spray
- 2 teaspoons powdered sugar

1. Preheat oven to 350°.

2. Beat granulated sugar and butter with a mixer at medium speed until well blended (about 5 minutes). Add molasses and egg, and beat well.

3. Lightly spoon flour into dry measuring cups, and level with a knife. Combine flour and next 5 ingredients, stirring well with a whisk. Add flour mixture to sugar mixture alternately with milk, beginning and ending with flour mixture.

4. Pour batter into an 8-inch square baking pan coated with cooking spray; sharply tap pan once on counter to remove air bubbles. Bake at 350° for 24 minutes or until a wooden pick inserted in center comes out clean. Cool in pan on wire rack. Sift powdered sugar over cake, and serve warm. Yield: 9 servings (serving size: 1 square).

CALORIES 196 (28% from fat); FAT 6.1g (sat 1.3g, mono 2.5g, poly 1.8g); PROTEIN 3.3g; CARB 32.1g; FIBER 0.5g; CHOL 24mg; IRON 1.6mg; SODIUM 158mg; CALC 55mg

A great dessert wine's sweetness comes across as refined, elegant, and well balanced by acidity. Above all, a first-rate dessert wine should never taste like the liquid version of bad wedding cake.

Chocolate Cheesecake

This silky cheesecake has a triple chocolate hit from a cookie crumb crust, cocoa, and semisweet chocolate chips.

W. & J. Graham's Vintage Port

  1   cup chocolate sandwich cookie crumbs (about 12 cookies)
  2   tablespoons sugar
  1   tablespoon butter, melted
Cooking spray
  ½   cup Dutch process cocoa
  ½   cup 2% low-fat milk
  3   ounces semisweet chocolate chips, melted
  3   (8-ounce) blocks fat-free cream cheese, softened
  2   (8-ounce) blocks ⅓-less-fat cream cheese, softened
1½   cups sugar
  3   tablespoons all-purpose flour
  2   teaspoons vanilla extract
  4   large eggs
Additional cookie crumbs (optional)

1. Preheat oven to 325°.

2. Combine first 3 ingredients; toss with a fork until moist. Press into bottom of a 9-inch springform pan coated with cooking spray.

3. Combine cocoa, milk, and chocolate; stir well with a whisk. Beat cheeses with a mixer at high speed until smooth. Add 1½ cups sugar, flour, and vanilla; beat well. Add chocolate mixture; beat well. Add eggs, 1 at a time, beating well after each addition. Pour cheese mixture into prepared pan; bake at 325° for 1 hour and 10 minutes or until almost set. Cheesecake is done when the center barely moves when the pan is touched. Remove from oven, and run a knife around outside edge. Cool to room temperature. Cover and chill at least 8 hours. Sprinkle with additional cookie crumbs, if desired. Yield: 16 servings (serving size: 1 wedge).

CALORIES 292 (36% from fat); FAT 11.8g (sat 6.7g, mono 0.9g, poly 0.2g); PROTEIN 12.4g; CARB 34.6g; FIBER 1.0g; CHOL 79mg; IRON 1.4mg; SODIUM 426mg; CALC 116mg

wine tip

The vintage Port that accompanies the chocolate cheesecake needs to be decanted, since such Ports "throw" a sediment (a harmless collection of color and tannin molecules that have dropped out of solution). Here's how:

1. Stand the bottle up a day or more before you plan to drink the Port to allow the sediment to settle to the bottom.

2. A few hours before you plan to drink the wine, remove the cork as slowly as possible, trying not to disturb the sediment.

3. Carefully pick the bottle up and gently begin pouring it slowly into a decanter or carafe. Stop when you see wisps of what looks like smoke in the wine (that's the sediment). There will probably be about an inch of wine left in the bottle.

Wine stewards often use a candle to backlight the wine during this process, but a candle isn't necessary as long as you pour very gently and slowly.

Poached Pears with Raspberry Sauce

Simply and quickly prepared in the microwave oven, these pears are topped with a colorful raspberry sauce. The sauce has a splash of balsamic vinegar and a sprinkling of pepper that help bring out the sweetness of the berries.

Müller-Catoir Haardter Bürgergarten Rieslaner Beerenauslese

    4 cups frozen unsweetened raspberries,
       thawed
    4 teaspoons honey
    2 teaspoons balsamic vinegar
    ¼ teaspoon freshly ground black pepper
    8 peeled firm Bosc pears (about
       3½ pounds)
    2 tablespoons lemon juice

1. Process raspberries in a food processor until smooth. Press raspberries through a fine sieve over a small bowl, reserving liquid; discard solids. Add honey, vinegar, and pepper to reserved raspberry liquid.
2. Rub pears with lemon juice. Place 4 pears in 2-quart casserole. Cover with lid. Microwave at HIGH 4 minutes or until pears are tender. Repeat with remaining 4 pears. To serve, drizzle sauce over pears. Yield: 8 servings (serving size: 1 pear and 2 tablespoons sauce).

CALORIES 239 (3% from fat); FAT 0.9g (sat 0g, mono 0.2g, poly 0.3g); PROTEIN 1.5g; CARB 61.1g; FIBER 4.4g; CHOL 0mg; IRON 1.3mg; SODIUM 2mg; CALC 38mg

Classic Sugar Cookies

Simplicity in its finest form, these tender sugar cookies are sweet, buttery, and irresistible.

Château d'Yquem Sauternes

1 cup all-purpose flour
¼ teaspoon baking soda
⅛ teaspoon salt
¼ cup butter, softened
⅔ cup sugar
1 teaspoon vanilla extract
1 large egg white
Cooking spray

1. Combine first 3 ingredients in a bowl; set aside. Beat butter with a mixer at medium speed until light and fluffy. Gradually add sugar, beating at medium speed until well blended. Add vanilla and egg white; beat well. Add flour mixture; stir until well blended. Turn dough out onto wax paper, and shape into a 6-inch log. Wrap in wax paper; freeze 3 hours or until dough is firm.

2. Preheat oven to 350°.

3. Cut log into 24 (¼-inch) slices, and place slices 1 inch apart on a baking sheet coated with cooking spray. Bake at 350° for 10 to 11 minutes. Remove from pan; cool on wire racks. Yield: 2 dozen (serving size: 1 cookie).

CALORIES 58 (31% from fat); FAT 2.0g (sat 1.0g, mono 0.8g, poly 0.1g); PROTEIN 0.7g; CARB 9.6g; FIBER 0.1g; CHOL 5mg; IRON 0.2mg; SODIUM 41mg; CALC 2mg

STYLES OF PORT, MADEIRA, AND SHERRY

Port, Madeira, and Sherry come in numerous styles, each of which tastes very different. While all Ports are sweet (and, therefore, are considered great dessert wines), only certain styles of Madeira and Sherry are sweet. Unless otherwise noted, all these wines should be served at cool temperature.

PORT

Port is made from any combination of five major grapes: touriga nacional, tinta barroca, tinto cão, touriga francesa, and tinta roriz. There are nine different styles of Port. Below are the major four Ports that are available in the United States.

Ruby and Ruby Reserve (sweet) Inexpensive and straightforward. Ruby Ports receive little bottle age before their release, but their ruby color and bold fruitiness are attractive. Ruby Reserves are the more powerful of these two Ports.

Tawny (sweet) Designated on the label as either 10, 20, 30, or 40 years old. Tawny Ports are blends of Ports from several years that are aged in the barrel a long time until they take on nutty, brown sugar, and vanilla flavors and a soft, silky texture.

Late Bottled Vintage (sweet) Known as LBVs. The most popular type of Port served in restaurants. These are Ports from a single vintage that have been aged in the barrel for four to six years and then bottled. Are ready to drink immediately. Do not need to be decanted.

Vintage (sweet) The most extraordinary type of Port and commensurately expensive. Made only in the best "declared" years. Vintage Ports are first aged two years in the barrel, to round off their powerful edges, and then can age a long time (decades) in bottles. Must be decanted before drinking (see page 157). A vintage Port from a renowned estate is known as a Single Quinta Vintage Port. *Quinta* means "farm" in Portuguese.

MADEIRA

The finest Madeiras are made from sercial, verdelho, bual, and malvasia (also known as malmsey) grapes. The name of the style takes its name from the grapes used. In addition to styles of Madeira, there are also several quality levels. In ascending order, they are 3-year-old and Rainwater, 5-year-old, 10-year-old, 15-year-old, Solera, and vintage Madeiras.

Sercial (dry) Made from sercial grapes grown in the coolest vineyards at the highest altitudes. Tangy and elegant, with bracing grip.

Verdelho (lightly sweet) Made from verdelho grapes grown in slightly warmer vineyards. More full-bodied than sercials.

Bual (medium-sweet) Made from bual grapes grown in warm vineyards. Concentrated and lushly rich.

Malmsey (sweet) Malvasia grapes are grown in the warmest locations closest to sea level, producing superripe grapes. A Madeira of astonishing richness.

SHERRY

All Sherries are made from palomino and/or Pedro Ximénez grapes.

Manzanilla (dry) A highly revered, light, elegant style of Sherry that only comes from a single tiny seaside Spanish town where the ocean air gives the wine a sea spray aroma and salty tang. Serve cold.

Fino (dry) Sherry at the apex of refinement and complexity. Fino has an unforgettable dry tang and aroma, reminiscent of a garden after a rain. Serve cold.

Amontillado (some dry; some medium-sweet) Tawny-colored and nutty tasting. Amontillados are rich and deeply complex wines evocative of hazelnuts roasted in butter.

Palo Cortado (some dry; some medium-sweet) A rare, eccentric type of Sherry. Palo cortados have the full body and lush texture of an oloroso and the hazelnut-like aroma of an amontillado.

Oloroso (some dry; most medium-sweet) A gorgeously aromatic long-aged Sherry with the voluptuous flavors of brown sugar, roasted nuts, vanilla, dried fruits, and caramel. Dark tawny in color.

Cream (sweet) Originally created for the British export market. Cream Sherries are usually very sweet. The best are rare, racy wines redolent of figs and roasted nuts.

Pedro Ximénez (sweet) As dark and dense as blackstrap molasses. Pedro Ximénez is one of the most intriguing sweet wines in the world.

SERVING DESSERT WINES

Here are the major dessert wines from around the world, as well as information about how to serve them. (Note that the dry styles of Madeira and Sherry are not included, since the dry styles are usually served as aperitifs or with savory dishes.) Though some dessert wines are traditionally served in specially designed glasses, the standard glass for white wine works fine for most dessert wines. The one exception is sweet (demi-sec) sparkling wine and Champagne, which should be served in a tall flute or tulip glass.

WINE	CHILL BOTTLE*	DECANT	SERVING SIZE**
Muscat including Orange Muscat, Black Muscat, Moscato, Moscato d'Asti, Muscat Canelli, and Muscat de Beaumes-de-Venise	yes	no	2 ounces
Sparkling Dessert Wines and Demi-Sec Champagnes	yes	no	4 ounces
Ice Wines and *Eiswein*	yes	no	2 ounces
Madeira Bual, Malmsey	during warm months, slightly chilled	no	2 to 4 ounces
Sherry Amontillado, Palo Cortado, Oloroso, Pedro Ximénez	no	no	2 to 3 ounces
Port Tawny Ruby, Ruby Reserve Late Bottled Vintage Vintage Single Quinta	slightly chilled no no no no	no no no yes yes	2 to 3 ounces 2 to 3 ounces 2 to 3 ounces 2 to 3 ounces 2 to 3 ounces
Australian Port-Style Wines Australian Fine Liqueur Tawny Australian Fortified Muscat and Tokay	no	no	2 to 3 ounces
Late Harvest White Wines and Botrytized Wines including Sauternes, Barsac, Late Harvest Riesling, German *Beerenauslese* (BA) and *Trockenbeerenauslese* (TBA), Late Harvest Semillon, Hungarian Tokaji Aszú, Austrian Ausbruch, Sweet Vouvray, Quarts de Chaume, Coteaux du Layon, Alsace Vendange Tardive, and Sélection de Grains Nobles	yes (with Tokaji Aszú, serve slightly chilled)	no	2 to 3 ounces
Late Harvest Reds including zinfandel	no	no	2 ounces
Dried Grapes including Vin Santo and Recioto della Valpolicella	no	no	2 ounces
Banyuls	yes	no	2 ounces

*__*No dessert wine should be served icy chilled.__ Most dessert wines taste best with a moderate chill of 45° to 55° F. One to two hours in the refrigerator should be sufficient. A wine that benefits from a very slight chill (such as tawny Port) can be put in the refrigerator for 10 to 20 minutes.*

*__**A standard 750-milliliter bottle contains approximately five 5-ounce servings.__ Thus, a typical serving of dessert wine is about half the amount you'd serve of a dry table wine. Note that many dessert wines come in 375-milliliter half bottles.*

Fisherman's Seafood Stew

rustic seafood supper

Sometimes, a bowl of warming soup, a hunk of hearty bread, and a glass of good wine are all you need on a cold winter's night—well, all that and a sweet duo to end the meal on an unforgettable note.

menu | wine

Fisherman's Seafood Stew

Ugly Bread

Toffee Blond Brownies

Serves 5

Every country around the Mediterranean region has a fisherman's stew, a chunky soup of fresh fish simmered in an herb- and garlic-scented tomato broth. Importantly, the fish is always humble—something a simple fisherman would cook for himself—with a firm "meaty" texture that doesn't fall apart in the hot broth.

Such stews also have traditional wine partners: bold, dry white wines and fruity, dry rosés. Rosés, in fact, are often preferred because they have more body than whites and so are more hearty as stew partners; also rosés work well with garlic and have an affinity for tomato broths. (There's also the fact that a red-tinged stew and a deep garnet-colored wine simply look great together, but I doubt the aesthetics are on most fishermen's minds.)

I love a dry rosé with this stew for all of the reasons above, plus the way rosé pairs with mussels. Mussels have a unique oceanic flavor that—though it sounds oxymoronic—is often a little earthy. As a result, mussels work well when there's a hint of red, earthy fruit in the wine. A rosé, which has both a red wine character and a white wine character, is the perfect partner. A wonderful dry rosé with this dish is **Zaca Mesa "Z Gris"** ($), from the Santa Ynez Valley of California. It's made from grenache and other Rhône grapes.

Madeira is one of the world's most sensual wines. It's hard to imagine a more knee-weakeningly luscious beverage. If you've never tasted Madeira, let a batch of these brownies be your excuse. Madeiras come in four main styles, from very dry to richly sweet (see page 160). **Blandy's 5 Year Old Malmsey Madeira** ($$) has a swirl of irresistible flavors—toffee, Tahitian vanilla, nuts roasted in butter, caramel, and brown sugar—that put it perfectly in sync with Toffee Blond Brownies.

Zaca Mesa "Z Gris" Rosé

Blandy's 5 Year Old Malmsey Madeira

Fisherman's Seafood Stew

This fast-cooking, tomato-flecked stew is brimming with fish and mussels. Be sure to use firm-fleshed fish that will hold together as the stew cooks.

Zaca Mesa "Z Gris" Rosé

- 2 tablespoons olive oil
- ½ cup minced shallots or onion
- ½ cup finely chopped red bell pepper
- ¾ cup dry white wine
- ½ teaspoon salt
- ½ teaspoon dried basil
- ¼ teaspoon black pepper
- 2 garlic cloves, minced
- 1 (14.5-ounce) can diced tomatoes, undrained
- 1 bay leaf
- 1 pound grouper, monkfish, or other firm whitefish fillets, cut into 5 pieces
- 1½ pounds small mussels, scrubbed and debearded
- 2 tablespoons chopped fresh flat-leaf parsley

1. Heat oil in a large Dutch oven over medium heat. Add shallots and bell pepper; cook 5 minutes. Add wine and next 6 ingredients; bring to a boil. Reduce heat; simmer 5 minutes, stirring occasionally.

2. Nestle fish into tomato mixture; top with mussels. Cover and cook 8 minutes; gently shake pan twice to stir mussels (do not lift cover). Discard any unopened shells and bay leaf. Sprinkle with parsley. Yield: 5 servings (serving size: about 2 ounces fish, ⅔ cup broth mixture, and about 8 mussels).

NOTE: Most mussels on the market come already scrubbed, purged with fresh water, and debearded. Mussels should be alive before they're cooked, so discard any broken shells or shells that won't close because open mussels are dead.

CALORIES 284 (30% from fat); FAT 9.6g (sat 1.6g,mono 4.9g, poly 1.6g); PROTEIN 35.3g; CARB 13.4g; FIBER 1.4g; CHOL 72mg; IRON 7.3mg; SODIUM 799mg; CALC 102mg

Ugly Bread

There is a communion of more than our bodies when bread is broken and wine is drunk.

—M.F.K. Fisher, American writer

Ugly Bread

Ugly is a term of endearment as well as a reference to a free-form shaped dough. This bread is shaped into a flat loaf rather than being baked in a pan.

Zaca Mesa "Z Gris" Rosé

1   package dry yeast (about
    2¼ teaspoons)
1   teaspoon sugar
1   cup warm water (100° to 110°)
3½ cups all-purpose flour, divided
¼   cup whole wheat flour
½   cup 1% low-fat milk
2   teaspoons olive oil
1   teaspoon salt
Cooking spray
1   tablespoon cornmeal

1. Dissolve yeast and sugar in warm water in a large bowl; let stand 5 minutes. Lightly spoon flours into dry measuring cups; level with a knife. Add 3 cups all-purpose flour, whole wheat flour, milk, oil, and salt to yeast mixture; stir with a wooden spoon until smooth. Turn dough out onto a floured surface. Knead until smooth and elastic (about 10 minutes); add some of remaining flour, 1 tablespoon at a time, to prevent dough from sticking to hands (dough will feel tacky).

2. Place dough in a large bowl coated with cooking spray, turning to coat top. Cover and let rise in a warm place (85°), free from drafts, 1 hour or until doubled in size. (Gently press two fingers into dough. If the indentation remains, dough has risen enough.) Punch dough down; cover and let rest 5 minutes. Divide dough in half.

3. Working with one portion at a time (cover remaining dough to keep from drying), shape each portion into a 6-inch oval on a floured surface. Cover with a slightly damp towel; let rise 20 minutes (dough will not double in size).

4. Working with one portion at a time, stretch into a 15-inch-long loaf (loaf will be flat); place on a baking sheet coated with cooking spray and sprinkled with cornmeal. Cover with a slightly damp towel; let rise 30 minutes (dough will not double in size). Uncover and lightly dust each loaf with remaining flour.

5. Preheat oven to 425°.

6. Bake at 425° for 25 minutes or until loaves are browned on bottom and sound hollow when tapped. Remove from pan; cool on wire racks. Yield: 2 loaves, 12 slices per loaf (serving size: 1 [1-inch] slice).

CALORIES 79 (8% from fat); FAT 0.7g (sat 0.1g, mono 0.3g, poly 0.1g); PROTEIN 2.4g; CARB 15.6g; FIBER 0.7g; CHOL 0.0mg; IRON 1mg; SODIUM 101mg; CALC 10mg

Toffee Blond Brownies

The toffee bits melt during baking and give these thin, gooey brownies a crunchy topping.

Blandy's 5 Year Old Malmsey Madeira

1   cup packed brown sugar
¼   cup butter, melted
¼   cup egg substitute
2   teaspoons vanilla extract
1   cup all-purpose flour
½   teaspoon baking powder
⅛   teaspoon salt
Cooking spray
¼   cup toffee baking bits (such as Heath)

1. Preheat oven to 350°.

2. Combine first 4 ingredients in a large bowl; stir with a whisk. Lightly spoon flour into a dry measuring cup; level with a knife. Combine flour, baking powder, and salt. Add flour mixture to sugar mixture; stir just until moist. Spread batter in an 8-inch square baking pan coated with cooking spray. Sprinkle with toffee bits. Bake at 350° for 22 minutes or until a wooden pick inserted in center comes out almost clean. Cool in pan on a wire rack. Yield: 12 servings.

CALORIES 168 (29% from fat); FAT 5.4g (sat 3.2g, mono 1.1g, poly 0.2g); PROTEIN 1.6g; CARB 28.4g; FIBER 0.3g; CHOL 14mg; IRON 1mg; SODIUM 120mg; CALC 31mg

wine tip

Madeira was the first American cult wine: Francis Scott Key sipped it while writing "The Star-Spangled Banner." George Washington's inauguration was toasted with it. And our Founding Fathers drank it as they signed the Declaration of Independence. For affluent families throughout the original colonies, Madeira parties were the height of fashion and were perhaps the forerunner of today's cocktail parties.

Madeira should be served in a good-sized white wine glass so that there's enough room to swirl the wine and take in those heady aromas. Serve Madeira at coolish room temperature, or in warm months give it the slightest chill.

If you don't finish the bottle, don't worry. An opened bottle of Madeira lasts for several months.

cozy cabin dinner

Often, the best holiday present is simply a reprieve from the hustle and bustle of the season. For me, that great gift means retreating far from the madding crowd and cooking something delicious for a few close friends. I love the way the heady aromas of these dishes fill the house and make everyone hungry—and nothing provides more inspiration to bring out several terrific wines.

menu | wine

Rich Mushroom Soup

Garlic-Rosemary Roasted Chicken

Spicy Sweet Potato Wedges

Fall Green Salad

Whole-grain loaves

Pumpkin-Orange Cake

Serves 8

Like Tracy and Hepburn, mushrooms and pinot noir are perfect partners. Mushrooms bring out pinot noir's most sensual quality: its primordial earthiness. In turn, pinot noir makes the corresponding earthiness of the mushrooms taste deeper, richer, and more profound. That the mushrooms come in the form of a creamy soup only accentuates the magnetlike attraction between the two. Since the soup is a first course, I like to serve it with a red Burgundy, generally the lightest bodied and silkiest of all the world's pinot noirs. If possible, opt for one ranked as a *Premier Cru.* Try **Domaine Jean Grivot Vosne-Romanée** ($$$$).

The French have elevated roasted chicken to a high art simply by slipping herbs and garlic beneath the skin and serving the chicken with a sumptuous red wine, usually from the south of France. The least-expensive and easiest-to-find southern French reds are called Côtes-du-Rhônes. If you opt for one, you'll find it a rustic and dependable partner for roasted chicken. Often, though, I prefer Côtes-du-Rhône's more sophisticated and muscular "big brother": Gigondas. Made primarily from grenache, mourvèdre, and syrah grapes, Gigondas is richly textured, spicy, and howling with deep red jammy flavors. One of my favorites is **Domaine Les Pallières Gigondas** ($$$).

The sweet earthiness of pumpkin, the citrusy zing of mandarin oranges, and the exotic tartness of pomegranate seeds make Pumpkin-Orange Cake nothing short of addictive as a winter treat. At the end of a great dinner party, it's smashing with **Quady "Essencia"** ($ for a 375-milliliter half bottle), from California.

Domaine Jean Grivot Vosne-Romanée

Domaine Les Pallières Gigondas

Quady "Essencia"

Garlic-Rosemary Roasted Chicken, Fall Green Salad,
Spicy Sweet Potato Wedges

Rich Mushroom Soup

This smooth and satisfying soup showcases the rich, earthy flavors of three different mushrooms.

Domaine Jean Grivot Vosne-Romanée

- 2 tablespoons all-purpose flour
- 1 cup boiling water
- 1 cup dried porcini mushrooms (about 1 ounce)
- 2 teaspoons butter
- 1½ cups chopped onion
- 2 teaspoons chopped garlic
- 2 teaspoons finely chopped fresh thyme
- ¼ teaspoon salt
- ¼ teaspoon freshly ground black pepper
- 6½ cups thinly sliced shiitake mushroom caps (about 1 pound mushrooms)
- 2 (8-ounce) packages sliced button mushrooms
- 4 cups fat-free, less-sodium chicken broth
- 1 cup 1% low-fat milk
- ½ cup half-and-half
- ¼ cup dry Amontillado Sherry

1. Place flour in a small skillet over medium-high heat; cook 2 minutes or until flour turns light brown, stirring constantly. Transfer flour to a small plate; cool.

2. Combine boiling water and porcini mushrooms in a bowl; cover and let steep 20 minutes. Strain porcini mushrooms through a sieve over a bowl, reserving soaking liquid. Chop mushrooms.

3. Melt butter in a Dutch oven over medium-high heat. Add onion; sauté 5 minutes or until tender. Add garlic, thyme, salt, and pepper; sauté 30 seconds. Add shiitake mushrooms; cook 3 minutes, stirring constantly. Add button mushrooms; cook 3 minutes, stirring constantly. Add chopped porcini mushrooms and broth to pan.

4. Combine reserved porcini soaking liquid and toasted flour, stirring with a whisk, and add to pan. Bring to a boil; reduce heat, and simmer, uncovered, 15 minutes. Add milk; simmer 10 minutes, stirring frequently. Remove from heat; stir in half-and-half and Sherry. Place 2 cups soup in a blender; process until smooth. Return pureed soup to pan. Warm the soup over low heat for 5 minutes or until thoroughly heated. Yield: 8 servings (serving size: 1 cup).

CALORIES 447 (29% from fat); FAT 14.5g (sat 5.0g, mono 4.2g, poly 2.1g); PROTEIN 36.8g; CARB 42.1g; FIBER 3.8g; CHOL 89mg; IRON 3.6mg; SODIUM 986mg; CALC 156mg

Garlic-Rosemary Roasted Chicken

It's amazing how the simple combination of garlic and rosemary can so infuse the chicken, making it taste every bit as glorious as it smells when cooking in the oven.

Domaine Les Pallières Gigondas

- 1 (6-pound) roasting chicken
- 1 tablespoon chopped fresh rosemary
- 4 garlic cloves, finely minced
- 2 medium red onions, quartered
- 2 whole garlic heads
- 2 teaspoons olive oil

1. Preheat oven to 450°.

2. Remove and discard giblets and neck from chicken. Rinse chicken under cold water; pat dry. Trim excess fat. Starting at neck cavity, loosen skin from breast and drumsticks by inserting fingers and gently pushing fingers between the skin and meat. Place rosemary and minced garlic beneath skin of breast and drumsticks. Lift wing tips up and over back; tuck under chicken. Place chicken, breast side up, on a broiler pan.

3. Cut a thin slice from end of each onion. Remove white papery skins from garlic heads (do not peel or separate cloves). Cut tops off garlic heads, leaving root end intact.

4. Insert meat thermometer into meaty part of thigh, making sure not to touch bone. Bake at 450° for 30 minutes. Brush onions and garlic heads with olive oil. Arrange onions and garlic heads around chicken. Reduce oven temperature to 350°; bake an additional 1 hour or until meat thermometer registers 180°. Cover chicken loosely with foil; let stand 10 minutes. Discard skin from chicken. Squeeze roasted heads of garlic to extract pulp; serve as a spread on French bread, if desired. Yield: 8 servings (serving size: 3 ounces chicken and 1 onion quarter).

CALORIES 231 (30% from fat); FAT 7.7g (sat 1.9g, mono 3.1g, poly 1.6g); PROTEIN 26.5g; CARB 13.5g; FIBER 2.7g; CHOL 76mg; IRON 1.4mg; SODIUM 78mg; CALC 50mg

Spicy Sweet Potato Wedges

These peppery sweet potatoes are delicious with roasted meats. Cooking them at a high heat makes their interior tender just as the sugar-and-spice coating begins to caramelize and brown them outside.

Domaine Les Pallières Gigondas

- 6 medium sweet potatoes
- Cooking spray
- 4 teaspoons sugar
- 1 teaspoon salt
- ½ teaspoon ground red pepper
- ¼ teaspoon black pepper

1. Preheat oven to 500°.

2. Peel potatoes; cut each lengthwise into 8 wedges. Place wedges in a large bowl; coat with cooking spray. Combine sugar, salt, and peppers, and sprinkle over potatoes, tossing well to coat. Arrange potatoes, cut sides down, in a single layer on a baking sheet. Bake at 500° for 25 minutes; turn wedges over. Bake an additional 15 to 20 minutes or until tender and beginning to brown. Yield: 8 servings (serving size: 6 wedges).

CALORIES 155 (0% from fat); FAT 0.1g (sat 0g, mono 0g, poly 0g); PROTEIN 2.7g; CARB 36.4g; FIBER 5.2g; CHOL 0mg; IRON 1.1mg; SODIUM 389mg; CALC 52mg

about the wine

Gigondas is a tiny charming village northeast of Châteauneuf-du-Pape. The name is derived from *jocunditas*—Latin for "joy" or "pleasantness"—which was the name given to the Gallo-Roman settlement that once occupied the spot Gigondas stands on today.

Fall Green Salad

Using three types of lettuce lends a variety of textures and flavors to this simple salad.

Domaine Les Pallières Gigondas

VINAIGRETTE:

¼ cup water
3 tablespoons fresh lemon juice
½ teaspoon cornstarch
1 tablespoon honey
½ teaspoon balsamic vinegar
¼ teaspoon salt
¼ teaspoon freshly ground black pepper
1 ounce shaved fresh Parmigiano-Reggiano cheese

SALAD:

4 cups torn curly leaf lettuce
4 cups torn romaine lettuce
3 cups trimmed arugula

1. To prepare the vinaigrette, combine water, juice, and cornstarch in a small saucepan, stirring with a whisk. Bring to a boil over medium-high heat; cook 1 minute, stirring frequently. Remove from heat. Stir in honey, vinegar, salt, and pepper. Place in a blender or food processor. Add cheese, and process until well blended. Cool to room temperature.

2. To prepare salad, place greens in a large bowl. Drizzle with vinaigrette, tossing gently to combine. Serve immediately. Yield: 8 servings (serving size: 1 cup).

CALORIES 38 (24% from fat); FAT 1.0g (sat 0.6g, mono 0.3g, poly 0.1g); PROTEIN 2.4g; CARB 5.9g; FIBER 1.4g; CHOL 2mg; IRON 0.5mg; SODIUM 145mg; CALC 80mg

Pumpkin-Orange Cake

You can also prepare this cake in a 13 x 9-inch pan (bake for 40 minutes, and cool in pan 10 minutes) or a tube pan (bake for 55 minutes, and cool in pan 20 minutes). For the variations, you'll need another pomegranate and an extra can of mandarin oranges for the topping.

Quady "Essencia"

½ cup granulated sugar
½ cup butter, softened
1 (15-ounce) can pumpkin
¼ cup egg substitute
½ teaspoon vanilla extract
2¾ cups sifted cake flour
1 teaspoon baking soda
½ teaspoon salt
½ teaspoon baking powder
½ teaspoon ground cinnamon
¼ teaspoon ground ginger
¼ teaspoon ground nutmeg
1 (12-ounce) can evaporated fat-free milk
Cooking spray
3 cups sifted powdered sugar, divided
¾ cup (6 ounces) ⅓-less-fat cream cheese, softened
1 teaspoon grated orange rind
2 cups mandarin oranges in light syrup, drained
1 cup pomegranate seeds (about 2 pomegranates)

1. Preheat oven to 350°.

2. Place granulated sugar and butter in a large bowl, and beat with a mixer at medium speed until well blended. Add pumpkin; beat well. Add egg substitute and vanilla; beat until well blended.

3. Lightly spoon flour into dry measuring cups; level with a knife. Combine flour and next 6 ingredients, stirring with a whisk. Add flour mixture and milk alternately to butter mixture, beginning and ending with flour mixture. Pour batter into 2 (9-inch) round cake pans coated with cooking spray; sharply tap pans once on counter to remove air bubbles. Bake at 350° for 30 minutes or until a wooden pick inserted in center comes out clean. Cool in pans 10 minutes on a wire rack; remove from pans. Cool completely on wire rack.

4. Place 1 cup powdered sugar and cream cheese in a large bowl; beat with a mixer at medium speed until well blended. Add 2 cups powdered sugar and rind; beat until fluffy.

5. Place 1 cake layer on a plate. Spread ⅔ cup cream cheese frosting over top. Top with remaining cake layer; spread remaining frosting over top, but not sides, of cake. Arrange orange slices in a ring around outer edge of top layer. Sprinkle pomegranate seeds over center of top layer. Store cake loosely covered in refrigerator. Yield: 14 servings (serving size: 1 slice).

CALORIES 338 (26% from fat); FAT 9.6g (sat 5.9g, mono 2.0g, poly 0.4g); PROTEIN 5.9g; CARB 58.5g; FIBER 1.2g; CHOL 28mg; IRON 2.3mg; SODIUM 354mg; CALC 102mg

about the wine

Orange muscat grapes, indigenous to the Mediterranean, are known as *moscato fior d'arancio* (orange blossom muscat). Wines made from orange muscat have a spicy orange-apricot character—and, as a result, have an affinity for orange-flavored cakes.

Pumpkin-Orange Cake

Beef Stew, Creamy Mashed
Potatoes

warm winter fare

Just as there are comfort foods, there are also comfort wines. Enjoying them together creates a deep sense of satisfaction ... of harmony ... of an experience enriched in a way that can't quite be put into words.

menu | wine

Beef Stew

Creamy Mashed Potatoes

Hearty Wheat Bread

Oatmeal-Walnut Cookies

Serves 6

The chill in the winter air makes me want to settle in for a warming dinner of my favorite comfort foods: stew and mashed potatoes. Aptly named comfort foods have a soothing effect—and certain wines are like this, too. I call them simply "comfort wines," and you don't have to think twice about understanding them. They're down-to-earth, homey, soul-satisfying, and perfectly easy to love.

To me, the greatest comfort wines in the world are Australian shirazes. Plush and ultrasoft red wines, they're as comfortable as flannel pajamas. Shiraz is the most famous red grape in Australia; you might know it by its European name of syrah. The beef stew featured here has a Mediterranean twist, incorporating stewed tomatoes and black olives that provide a delicious contrast to the meaty sweetness of the beef. The shiraz's hints of menthol pick up on the olivey brininess in a fascinating way, heightening the overall complexity of experiencing the food and wine together. Of course, any wine intended for beef stew needs to have considerable body and richness—**St. Hallett "Faith" Shiraz** ($$), from Australia's Barossa Valley, possesses both.

Many of us never get beyond coffee as a companion for cookies. But If you want to raise the bar and turn these Oatmeal-Walnut Cookies into an otherworldly experience, serve them with a sweet PX Sherry from Spain made from Pedro Ximénez (PX) grapes. Be prepared: PX Sherries are as syrupy and dark as molasses, with brown sugar, chocolate, and toffee flavors that are deliciously unreal. For one of the most extraordinary and hedonistic wine experiences you'll ever have, try **Bodegas Toro Albalá, Pedro Ximénez Gran Reserva Sherry** ($$$$). Since the wine is aged for decades in oak barrels, the current vintages now in the marketplace are from the 1970s and 1980s!

St. Hallett "Faith" Shiraz

Bodegas Toro Albalá, Pedro Ximénez Gran Reserva Sherry

Beef Stew

Serve this Mediterranean-inspired stew over Creamy Mashed Potatoes. Make and keep warm in a Dutch oven or slow cooker.

St. Hallett "Faith" Shiraz

1½   teaspoons olive oil
1½   pounds beef stew meat, cut into 1-inch pieces
3½   cups halved mushrooms (about 8 ounces)
 2   cups diagonally cut carrot
1½   cups coarsely chopped onion
1½   cups sliced celery
 2   garlic cloves, minced
1½   cups less-sodium beef broth
 1   cup syrah/shiraz
1¼   teaspoons kosher salt
 ½   teaspoon dried thyme
 ¼   teaspoon coarsely ground black pepper
 2   (14.5-ounce) cans no-salt-added stewed tomatoes, undrained
 2   bay leaves
 ½   cup oil-cured black olives, pitted and sliced
 1   tablespoon balsamic vinegar
 ¼   cup chopped fresh flat-leaf parsley

1. Heat oil in a large Dutch oven over medium-high heat. Add beef; cook 5 minutes, browning on all sides. Remove from pan. Add mushrooms and next 4 ingredients to pan; cook 5 minutes, stirring occasionally. Return beef to pan. Stir in broth and next 6 ingredients; bring to a boil. Cover, reduce heat, and simmer 1 hour. Stir in olives, and cook 30 minutes or until beef is tender. Discard bay leaves. Stir in vinegar. Sprinkle with parsley. Yield: 6 servings (serving size: 1⅓ cups).

CALORIES 282 (33% from fat); FAT 10.4g (sat 3.3g, mono 5.1g, poly 0.6g); PROTEIN 25.4g; CARB 20.7g; FIBER 5.1g; CHOL 72mg; IRON 5.3mg; SODIUM 723mg; CALC 113mg

Creamy Mashed Potatoes

Yukon golds are yellow-fleshed potatoes that have a naturally buttery flavor, which enhances their rich creaminess.

St. Hallett "Faith" Shiraz

2¼   pounds cubed peeled Yukon gold potato
 ⅔   cup 2% reduced-fat milk, warmed
 2   tablespoons butter, softened
 1   teaspoon kosher salt
 ¼   teaspoon coarsely ground black pepper

1. Place potatoes in a saucepan; cover with water. Bring to a boil. Reduce heat, and simmer 15 minutes or until tender. Drain. Return potatoes to pan. Add milk and remaining ingredients; mash to desired consistency. Cook over low heat until warm. Yield: 8 servings (serving size: ⅔ cup).

CALORIES 174 (28% from fat); FAT 5.5g (sat 3.4g, mono 1.4g, poly 0.2g); PROTEIN 3.2g; CARB 28.6g; FIBER 1.9g; CHOL 15mg; IRON 0.5mg; SODIUM 315mg; CALC 29mg

Hearty Wheat Bread

Coffee and stout give this wheat bread richness, heartiness, and a hint of espresso-like bitterness.

St. Hallett "Faith" Shiraz

 ½   cup warm strong brewed coffee (100° to 110°)
 ½   cup warm Guinness Stout (100° to 110°)
 1   package dry yeast (about 2¼ teaspoons)
 1   cup whole wheat flour
 ¼   cup toasted wheat germ
 1   cup bread flour, divided
1⅛   teaspoons salt
Cooking spray
 1   tablespoon cornmeal

1. Combine coffee and stout in a large bowl. Dissolve yeast in coffee mixture; let stand 5 minutes. Lightly spoon whole wheat flour into a dry measuring cup; level with a knife. Add whole wheat flour and wheat germ to yeast mixture; stir well to combine. Cover and let stand at room temperature 30 minutes to create a sponge (mixture will rise slightly and bubbles will form across the surface).

2. Lightly spoon bread flour into dry measuring cups; level with a knife. Stir ¾ cup bread flour and salt into sponge; stir until a soft dough forms. Turn dough out onto a floured surface. Knead until smooth and elastic (about 8 minutes); add enough of remaining bread flour, 1 tablespoon at a time, to prevent dough from sticking to hands (dough will feel slightly tacky).

3. Place dough in a large bowl coated with cooking spray, turning to coat top. Cover and let rise a second time in a warm place (85°), free from drafts, 45 minutes or until doubled in size. (Gently press two fingers into dough. If indentation remains, dough has risen enough.) Punch dough down. Cover and let rise in a warm place (85°), free from drafts, 30 minutes or until doubled in size. Punch dough down; cover and let rest for 5 minutes. Shape dough into an 8-inch oval; place on a baking sheet sprinkled with 1 tablespoon cornmeal. Lightly coat surface of dough with cooking spray. Cover and let rise in a warm place (85°), free from drafts, 15 minutes or until doubled in size.

4. Preheat oven to 400°.

5. Uncover dough, and cut a shallow ¼-inch slash down center of loaf. Bake at 400° for 20 minutes or until loaf is browned on bottom and sounds hollow when tapped. Cool on a wire rack. Yield: 10 servings (serving size: 1 slice).

CALORIES 99 (5% from fat); FAT 0.6g (sat 0.1g, mono 0.1g, poly 0.3g); PROTEIN 4.5g; CARB 20.3g; FIBER 2.4g; CHOL 0mg; IRON 1.5mg; SODIUM 268mg; CALC 7mg

Hearty Wheat Bread

Oatmeal-Walnut Cookies

Golden raisins and walnuts add sweetness and crunch to a basic oatmeal cookie.

Bodegas Toro Albalá, Pedro Ximénez Gran Reserva Sherry

- ½ cup granulated sugar
- ⅓ cup packed dark brown sugar
- ¼ cup butter, softened
- 1 teaspoon vanilla extract
- 1 large egg
- ¾ cup all-purpose flour
- 1 cup regular oats
- ¼ teaspoon salt
- ⅔ cup golden raisins
- ¼ cup chopped toasted walnuts

Cooking spray

1. Preheat oven to 350°.

2. Place first 5 ingredients in a large bowl. Beat with a mixer at medium speed until well blended. Lightly spoon flour into a dry measuring cup; level with a knife. Add flour, oats, and salt to egg mixture; beat well. Stir in raisins and walnuts.

3. Drop by level tablespoons, 1½ inches apart, onto a baking sheet coated with cooking spray. Bake at 350° for 12 minutes or until lightly browned. Remove from oven; let stand 2 minutes. Remove cookies from baking sheet; serve warm. Yield: 2 dozen (serving size: 1 cookie).

NOTE: You can make these ahead of time and store them in an airtight container, but they're best served warm.

CALORIES 109 (28% from fat); FAT 3.4g (sat 1.4g, mono 0.9g, poly 0.9g); PROTEIN 2.1g; CARB 18.3g; FIBER 1.1g; CHOL 14mg; IRON 0.7mg; SODIUM 24mg; CALC 12mg

about the wine

If Sherry makes you think of your grandmother, then your grandmother must be one pretty hip woman. Sherry is *in*—and it's sensational with food. It's my favorite wine with Oatmeal-Walnut Cookies, but it's not simply a single wine. Instead, Sherry comes in seven definitive styles (see the chart on page 160), from bone dry to richly sweet.

The Sherry I adore with these cookies is Pedro Ximénez—the sweetest style of Sherry, made from Pedro Ximénez grapes. (The ultrasweet juice of these grapes is also used to lightly sweeten other types of Sherry.) Most Pedro Ximénez Sherries are nearly black in color and have a texture thicker than cough syrup. To achieve this degree of sweetness and intensity, the grapes are picked and then laid out under the scorching sun for two to three weeks to dry and shrivel. Only when the sugar in them becomes concentrated are the grapes slowly fermented into wine.

A thimbleful is more than a dessert wine—it's dessert. This Sherry also tastes great slathered over vanilla or coffee-flavored ice cream.

Pork Cassoulet

french country dinner

No dish is more French than cassoulet, a long-simmered stew that vaults humble ingredients into the stratosphere of sophistication. Served with a showstopper wine, cassoulet highlights an unforgettable evening shared with friends.

menu | wine

Pork Cassoulet

Classic French Bread

French cheese plate

Serves 10

Cassoulet is a specialty of Alsace, a wine region in eastern France known for its tranquil beauty, extraordinary wines, and phenomenal cuisine. Because cassoulet is their local dish, Alsatians have centuries of experience pairing it with wine. Their top choice—and mine—is a dry Alsace riesling. Like a bolt of lightening, riesling cuts through the richness of the pork and the savoriness of the slow-cooked beans. To make this dinner truly unforgettable, serve a top riesling, such as **Domaine Zind Humbrecht "Gueberschwihr" Riesling** ($$$), one of the most intense and pure expressions of white wine that I've ever tasted.

After such a substantial dish as cassoulet, a rich dessert is just too over the top. I prefer to serve a plate of cheeses along with some fruits or nuts. Most cheeses are fairly salty and/or acidic, making a successful wine-and-cheese pairing difficult. By adding something sweet—such as a few slices of fig, plum, or pear; a few berries; or some glazed walnuts or roasted almonds—you can balance the cheeses' saltiness and acidity to create a "bridge" to the wine. I love to serve three irresistible French cheeses: Crottin de Chavignol (from goats' milk), Brin d'Amour (from sheep's milk), and Pierre Robert (from cows' milk). Be sure they are served at room temperature for maximum flavor and texture.

As it happens, the Domaine Zind Humbrecht Riesling is extraordinary with these cheeses, so one wine is all you need for this entire menu. But if I'm going for the all-out, can't-top-this, wow experience, I serve the cheese plate with a second Alsace wine, **Domaine Weinbach Muscat Réserve** ($$$$), which is bone dry but breathtaking in its pure incisive fruitiness. It's one of the greatest and most exotic wines of France—and simply stellar with these cheeses.

Domaine Zind Humbrecht "Gueberschwihr" Riesling

Domaine Weinbach Muscat Réserve

Pork Cassoulet

A traditional French cassoulet is meant to be served the day after it's cooked because the separate ingredients meld overnight to create a dish with deep, rich flavor.

Domaine Zind Humbrecht "Gueberschwihr" Riesling

1 pound dried Great Northern beans
2 bacon slices, cut into 1-inch pieces
3 pounds boneless pork loin, cut into 1-inch cubes
1 pound turkey kielbasa, cut into ½-inch slices
2½ cups chopped onion
1 cup sliced celery
1 cup (¼-inch) sliced carrot
4 garlic cloves, minced
2 teaspoons dried thyme
½ cup Alsace riesling
¼ cup water
2 tablespoons tomato paste
½ teaspoon salt
¼ teaspoon black pepper
1 (14-ounce) can no-salt-added diced tomatoes, undrained
1 (14½-ounce) can fat-free, less-sodium chicken broth
1 cup (¼-inch-thick) red bell pepper rings
1½ cups (1-inch) cubed French bread
⅓ cup (about 1½ ounces) grated fresh Parmesan cheese

1. Sort and wash beans, and place in a large Dutch oven. Cover with water to 2 inches above beans; bring to a boil, and cook 2 minutes. Remove from heat; cover and let stand 1 hour. Drain; return beans to pan. Cover beans with water; bring to a boil. Cover, reduce heat, and simmer 20 minutes; drain and set aside.
2. Preheat oven to 300°.
3. Add bacon to pan; cook over medium heat until crisp. Remove bacon with a slotted spoon, and crumble. Increase heat to medium-high. Add pork to drippings in pan; cook 5 minutes or until browned,

stirring occasionally. Remove pork with a slotted spoon. Add kielbasa to pan; cook 5 minutes or until browned, stirring occasionally. Remove kielbasa with a slotted spoon. Add onion, celery, carrot, garlic, and thyme to pan; sauté 4 minutes or until tender. Stir in wine, ¼ cup water, tomato paste, salt, pepper, tomatoes, and broth.
4. Return beans, bacon, pork, and kielbasa to pan; bring to a boil. Cover and bake at 300° for 1 hour. Arrange bell pepper rings over top.
5. Place bread in a food processor; pulse 10 times or until coarse crumbs form to measure 1½ cups. Combine breadcrumbs and cheese. Sprinkle cassoulet with breadcrumb mixture. Return cassoulet to oven; bake, uncovered, an additional 45 minutes. Yield: 10 servings (serving size: about 1½ cups).

CALORIES 526 (30% from fat); FAT 17.6g (sat 6.5g, mono 7.3g, poly 2.5g); PROTEIN 50.7g; CARB 40.8g; FIBER 11.5g; CHOL 117mg; IRON 5.1mg; SODIUM 808mg; CALC 193mg

Classic French Bread

I'm certainly in favor of the European style of stopping off at the bakery for a fresh-baked baguette on the way home. But if you're a baker at heart, here's a no-fail recipe for a classic bread.

Domaine Zind Humbrecht "Gueberschwihr" Riesling

1 package dry yeast (about 2¼ teaspoons)
1 cup warm water (100° to 110°)
3 cups bread flour
1 teaspoon salt
Cooking spray
1 tablespoon water
1 large egg white

1. Dissolve yeast in 1 cup warm water in a small bowl; let stand 5 minutes.
2. Lightly spoon flour into dry measuring cups; level with a knife. Place flour and salt in a food processor, and pulse 2 times or

until blended. With food processor on, slowly add yeast mixture through food chute, and process until dough forms a ball. Process for an additional 1 minute. Turn dough out onto a lightly floured surface, and knead lightly 4 or 5 times.
3. Place dough in a large bowl coated with cooking spray, turning to coat top. Cover and let rise in a warm place (85°), free from drafts, 45 minutes or until doubled in size.
4. Punch dough down, and shape into a 6-inch round loaf. Place loaf on a baking sheet coated with cooking spray. Cover dough, and let rise 30 minutes or until doubled in size.
5. Preheat oven to 450°.
6. Uncover dough, and make 3 (¼-inch-deep) diagonal cuts across top of loaf using a sharp knife. Combine 1 tablespoon water and egg white, and brush mixture over top of loaf. Bake at 450° for 20 minutes or until loaf sounds hollow when tapped. Yield: 12 servings (serving size: 1 slice).

CALORIES 127 (5% from fat); FAT 0.7g (sat 0.1g, mono 0.1g, poly 0.3g); PROTEIN 4.6g; CARB 25.1g; FIBER 0.2g; CHOL 0mg; IRON 1.6mg; SODIUM 200mg; CALC 6mg

entertaining tip

Besides featuring fresh fruits, cheese plates in France, Spain, and Italy often include a puddle of wildflower honey, a fruit "paste" (such as quince paste) called *membrillo,* or small slivers of a dense torte made of dried fruits and honey. All are elegant and work wonderfully with wine. Quince paste and dried fruit tortes can be found in most good cheese shops.

about the wine

Alsace rieslings are medium bodied, intensely flavored, and always dry. They are also one of the most food-flexible wines in the world. On the one hand, rieslings are just the ticket with such citrusy, exotic, bold dishes as Citrus Chicken Tagine (see "Autumn," page 131). At the same time, they are traditional and soul-satisfyingly delicious with slow-cooked pork dishes, such as a cassoulet.

Classic French Bread

true romance

With all due respect to flowers, a fabulous dinner featuring seductive wines, sumptuous dishes, and a sublime superchocolaty dessert is just about the best Valentine's gift ever.

menu | wine

Roasted Beet, Pistachio, and Pear Salad

***

Roasted Salmon and Leeks in Phyllo Packets

French bread

***

Chocolate-Chunk Bread Puddings

Serves 2

For me, the most luxurious (and appropriate) wine to begin Valentine's Day evening is a pink-tinged rosé sparkling wine. Nothing creates the right romantic mood better. Rosé sparklers are rarer, more exquisite, and more difficult to make than golden sparkling wines. They're also flat-out sensational with Roasted Beet, Pistachio, and Pear Salad. The red fruit character of the bubbly picks up perfectly with the beets; the hints of pear in the wine are underscored by the pears in the salad; the pistachios echo the bubbly's nuttiness; and to top it off, the honey in the dressing balances the sparkler's vibrant crispness. A knockout rosé sparkler with aromas and flavors evocative of crushed raspberries, crème brûlée, custard, and whipped cream is **Gloria Ferrer Brut Rosé** ($$$), from the Carneros region of California.

With romance as the subtext and salmon as the dish, the next wine to serve can only be a pinot noir. For centuries, pinot noir has been considered the most sensual of red grapes, thanks to its supple, silky texture and earthy, sexy scent. As it happens, pinot noir is also considered a classic match for salmon. The richest of fish needs a counterbalance, and pinot noir's underlying acidity deliciously provides it. A sublime pinot noir is **Sea Smoke "Southing" Pinot Noir** ($$$$), from California's Santa Rita Hills.

With these utterly hedonistic chocolate bread puddings, the single best wine is Port (see the chart on page 160). I often serve a Late Bottled Vintage Port (LBV) with this menu. Juicy and very berried, LBVs are supple and bold at the same time and do not require any special aging or decanting. Try the impeccable **Ramos Pinto Late Bottled Vintage Port** ($$), from Portugal.

Gloria Ferrer Brut Rosé Sparkling Wine

Sea Smoke "Southing" Pinot Noir

Ramos Pinto Late Bottled Vintage Port

Roasted Salmon and Leeks
in Phyllo Packets

Roasted Beet, Pistachio, and Pear Salad

The vibrant beets lend a pink hue to the pears, which sets the mood for Valentine's Day. You can prepare the salad early in the day and scoop it onto lettuce leaves just before serving.

Gloria Ferrer Brut Rosé Sparkling Wine

    2 beets (about ¾ pound)
    1 cup diced Asian pear or ripe pear
   ¼ cup diced celery
    2 tablespoons chopped pistachios
    3 tablespoons fresh lemon juice
    1 tablespoon honey
   ½ teaspoon brown sugar
   ¼ teaspoon black pepper
Dash of salt
Dash of ground red pepper
    2 curly leaf lettuce leaves (optional)

1. Preheat oven to 425°.
2. Leave root and 1 inch of stem on beets; scrub with a brush. Place beets in a small baking dish. Bake at 425° for 50 minutes or until tender. Cool. Trim off beet roots; rub off skins. Dice beets.
3. Combine beets, pear, celery, and pistachios in a medium bowl.
4. Combine juice and next 5 ingredients, stirring well with a whisk. Drizzle over beet mixture, tossing gently to coat.
5. Serve at room temperature on lettuce leaves, if desired. Yield: 2 servings (serving size: 1 cup).

CALORIES 153 (22% from fat); FAT 3.8g (sat 0.4g, mono 1.9g, poly 1.1g); PROTEIN 3.6g; CARB 29.9g; FIBER 4.3g; CHOL 0mg; IRON 1.4mg; SODIUM 147mg; CALC 41mg

Roasted Salmon and Leeks in Phyllo Packets

As leeks, carrots, and tarragon steam-roast with the fish, the phyllo locks in the flavors and crisps on the outside to form a delicate, crunchy coating. This dish is similar to those cooked *en papillote* (in parchment), but in this case the wrapping is edible.

Sea Smoke "Southing" Pinot Noir

   ½ cup (2-inch) julienne-cut leek
   ½ cup (2-inch) julienne-cut carrot
    2 teaspoons minced fresh tarragon
   ½ teaspoon salt, divided
    4 (6-ounce) salmon fillets (about 1 inch thick)
   ⅛ teaspoon freshly ground black pepper
   12 (18 x 14-inch) sheets frozen phyllo dough, thawed and divided
Cooking spray
    2 teaspoons fresh lemon juice, divided
    4 lemon wedges
Tarragon sprigs (optional)

1. Preheat oven to 400°.
2. Cook leek and carrot in boiling water 1 minute; drain. Combine leek mixture, tarragon, and ¼ teaspoon salt in a small bowl, tossing gently. Sprinkle salmon evenly with ¼ teaspoon salt and pepper.
3. Place 1 phyllo sheet on a large cutting board or work surface (cover remaining phyllo dough to prevent drying); lightly coat with cooking spray. Repeat layers twice, ending with phyllo. Gently press phyllo layers together. Lightly coat top phyllo sheet with cooking spray. Arrange ¼ cup leek mixture along center of 1 short edge of phyllo, leaving a 4-inch border; top with 1 fillet. Drizzle with ½ teaspoon lemon juice. Fold long edges of phyllo over fish.
4. Starting at short edge with 4-inch border, roll up jelly-roll fashion. Place wrapped fish, seam sides down, on a baking sheet coated with cooking spray. Lightly coat wrapped fish with cooking

spray. Repeat procedure with remaining phyllo dough, cooking spray, leek mixture, salmon, and juice.
5. Bake at 400° for 15 minutes or until lightly browned, and let stand 5 minutes before serving. Serve with lemon wedges. Garnish with tarragon sprigs, if desired. Yield: 4 servings (serving size: 1 packet).

CALORIES 457 (32% from fat); FAT 16.5g (sat 3.9g, mono 7.5g, poly 3.7g); PROTEIN 40.6g; CARB 33.4g; FIBER 1.8g; CHOL 87mg; IRON 2.4mg; SODIUM 656mg; CALC 40mg

about the wine

Rosé Champagnes and sparkling wines have always been the ultimate connoisseurs' wines. Rare, fairly expensive, bone dry, and painstaking to make, rosé sparklers are also quintessentially sensual. Indeed, from a taste standpoint, rose sparklers are usually richer, fuller, and more opulently fruity than golden sparkling wines. And because they have more body, they have the weight and power to complement an amazing diversity of dishes.

Chocolate-Chunk Bread Puddings

Try not to chop the chocolate too finely so you'll have good-sized chunks. You can use challah or brioche instead of the Hawaiian sweet bread.

Ramos Pinto Late Bottled Vintage Port

1¾ cups (½-inch) cubed Hawaiian sweet bread
⅔ cup 2% reduced-fat milk
2 tablespoons sugar
1½ tablespoons unsweetened cocoa
1 tablespoon Kahlúa (coffee-flavored liqueur)
½ teaspoon vanilla extract
1 large egg, lightly beaten
Cooking spray
1 ounce semisweet chocolate, coarsely chopped
2 tablespoons whipped cream or canned whipped topping

1. Preheat oven to 350°.
2. Arrange bread cubes in a single layer on a baking sheet. Bake at 350° for 5 minutes or until toasted. Remove bread from oven; reduce oven temperature to 325°.
3. Combine milk and next 5 ingredients in a medium bowl, stirring well with a whisk. Add bread, tossing gently to coat. Cover and chill 30 minutes or up to 4 hours.
4. Divide half of bread mixture evenly between 2 (6-ounce) ramekins or custard cups coated with cooking spray; sprinkle evenly with half of chocolate. Divide remaining bread mixture between ramekins; top with remaining chocolate.
5. Place ramekins in an 8-inch square baking pan; add hot water to pan to a depth of 1 inch. Bake at 325° for 35 minutes or until set. Serve warm with whipped cream. Yield: 2 servings (serving size: 1 pudding and 1 tablespoon whipped cream).

CALORIES 323 (30% from fat); FAT 10.7g (sat 5.2g, mono 1.6g, poly 0.4g); PROTEIN 10.6g; CARB 4.0g; FIBER 1.9g; CHOL 117mg; IRON 2.2mg; SODIUM 219mg; CALC 147mg

Wine makes every meal an occasion, every table more elegant, every day more civilized.

—André Simon, French wine authority

index

Specific wine names and varietals are indicated in *italics*.

credits

The editors would like to thank the following companies and
organizations for their assistance in producing this book:

Classic Wine Company, Birmingham, AL
Embassy of Spain, New York, NY
Screwpull Ltd., Le Creuset, Andover, Hampshire, UK
Village Wine Market, Birmingham, AL
Wilson Daniels Ltd., St. Helena, CA
The Wine Cellar, Birmingham, AL